AMERICAN CLASSICS

COLONIAL DAMES
AND
GOOD WIVES

Alice Morse Earle

FREDERICK UNGAR PUBLISHING CO.
NEW YORK

83805

Republished 1962

Printed in the
United States of America

Library of Congress
Catalog Card No. 62-9682

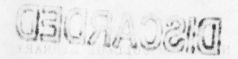

917.3
Ear

CONTENTS

COLONIAL DAMES AND GOODWIVES.

CHAPTER I.

CONSORTS AND RELICTS.

IN the early days of the colony of Massachusetts Bay, careful lists were sent
back to old England by the magistrates, telling what "to provide to send to New England" in order to ensure the successful
planting and tender nourishing of the new
settlement. The earliest list includes such
homely items as "benes and pese," tame
turkeys, copper kettles, all kinds of useful
apparel and wholesome food; but the list is
headed with a most significant, a typically
Puritan item, *Ministers*. The list sent to
the Emigration Society by the Virginian
colonists might equally well have been
headed, to show their most crying need,
with the word *Wives*.

The settlement of Virginia bore an entirely
different aspect from that of New England.
It was a community of men who planted
Jamestown. There were few women among
the early Virginians. In 1608 one Mistress
Forrest came over with a maid, Anne Bur-
raws, who speedily married John Laydon, the
first marriage of English folk in the new
world. But wives were few, save squaw-wives,
therefore the colony did not thrive. Sir
Edwin Sandys, at a meeting of the Emigration Society in London, in November, 1619,
said that "though the colonists are seated
there in their persons some four years, they
are not settled in their minds to make it
their place of rest and continuance." They
all longed to gather gold and to return to
England as speedily as possible, to leave
that state of "solitary uncouthness," as one
planter called it. Sandys and that delightful gentleman, the friend and patron of
Shakespeare, the Earl of Southampton,
planned, as an anchor in the new land, to
send out a cargo of wives for these planters,
that the plantation might "grow in genera-
tions and not be pieced out from without."
In 1620 the Jonathan and the London Mer-

chant brought ninety maids to Virginia on a venture, and a most successful venture it proved.

There are some scenes in colonial life which stand out of the past with much clearness of outline, which seem, though no details survive, to present to us a vivid picture. One is this landing of ninety possible wives — ninety homesick, seasick but timidly inquisitive English girls — on Jamestown beach, where pressed forward, eagerly and amorously waiting, about four hundred lonely emigrant bachelors — bronzed, sturdy men, in leather doublets and breeches and cavalier hats, with glittering swords and bandoleers and fowling-pieces, without doubt in their finest holiday array, to choose and secure one of these fair maids as a wife. Oh, what a glorious and all-abounding courting, a mating-time, was straightway begun on the Virginian shore on that happy day in May. A man needed a quick eye, a ready tongue, a manly presence, if he were to succeed against such odds in supply and demand, and obtain a fair one, or indeed any one, from this bridal array. But whosoever he won was indeed a prize, for all were asserted to be " young, handsome, honestly educated maids, of honest life and carriage" — what more could any man desire ? Gladly did the husband pay to the Emigration Company the one hundred and twenty pounds of leaf tobacco, which formed, in one sense, the purchase money for the wife. This was then valued at about eighty dollars : certainly a man in that matrimonial market got his money's worth ; and the complaining colonial chronicler who asserted that ministers and milk were the only cheap things in New England, might have added — and wives the only cheap things in Virginia.

It was said by old writers that some of these maids were seized by fraud, were trapanned in England, that unprincipled spirits "took up rich yeomans' daughters to serve his Majesty as breeders in Virginia unless they paid money for their release." This trapanning was one of the crying abuses of the day, but in this case it seems scarcely present. For the girls appear to have been given a perfectly fair showing in all this barter. They were allowed to marry no irresponsible men, to go nowhere as servants, and, indeed, were not pressed to marry at all if against their wills. They were to be "housed lodged and provided for of diet" until they decided to accept a husband. Naturally nearly all did marry, and from the unions with these young, handsome and godly-carriaged maids sprang many of our respected Virginian families.

No coquetry was allowed in this mating. A girl could not promise to marry two men, under pain of fine or punishment; and at least one presumptuous and grasping man was whipped for promising marriage to two girls at the same time — as he deserved to be when wives were so scarce.

Other ship-loads of maids followed, and with the establishment of these Virginian families was dealt, as is everywhere else that the family exists, a fatal blow at a community of property and interests, but the colony flourished, and the civilization of the new world was begun. For the unit of society may be the individual, but the molecule of civilization is the family. When men had wives and homes and children they "sett down satysfied" and no longer sighed for England. Others followed quickly and eagerly ; in three years thirty-five hundred emigrants had gone from England to Virginia, a marked contrast to the previous years of uncertainty and dissatisfaction.

Virginia was not the only colony to import wives for its colonists. In 1706 His Majesty Louis XIV. sent a company of twenty young girls to the Governor of Louisiana, Sieur de Bienville, in order to consolidate his colony. They were to be given good homes, and to be well married, and it was thought they would soon teach the Indian squaws many useful domestic employments. These young girls were of unspotted reputation, and upright lives, but they did not love their new homes ; a dispatch of the Governor says : —

The men in the colony begin through habit to use corn as an article of food, but the women, who are mostly Parisians, have for this kind of food a dogged aversion which has not been subdued. Hence they inveigh bitterly against his Grace the Bishop of Quebec who they say has enticed them away from home under pretext of sending them to enjoy the milk and honey of the land of promise.

I don't know how this venture succeeded, but I cannot fancy anything more like the personification of incompatibility, of inevitable failure, than to place these young Parisian women (who had certainly known of the manner of living of the court of Louis XIV.) in a wild frontier settlement, and to expect them to teach Western squaws any domestic or civilized employment, and then to make them eat Indian corn, which they loathed as do the Irish peasants. Indeed, they were to be pitied. They rebelled and threatened to run away — whither I cannot guess, nor what they would eat save Indian corn if they did run away — and they stirred up such a dissatisfaction that the imbroglio was known as the Petticoat Rebellion, and the governor was much jeered at for his unsuccessful wardship and his attempted matrimonial agency.

In 1721 eighty young girls were landed in Louisiana as wives, but these were not godly-carriaged young maids ; they had been taken from Houses of Correction, especially from Paris. In 1728 came another company known as *filles à la cassette*, or casket girls, for each was given by the French government a casket of clothing to carry to the new home ; and in later years it became a matter of much pride to Louisianians that their descent was from the casket-girls, rather than from the correction-girls.

Another wife-market for the poorer class of wifeless colonists was afforded through the white bond-servants who came in such numbers to the colonies. They were of three classes; convicts, free-willers or redemptioners, and "kids" who had been stolen and sent to the new world, and sold often for a ten years' term of service.

Maryland, under the Baltimores, was the sole colony that not only admitted convicts, but welcomed them. The labor of the branded hand of the malefactor, the education and accomplishments of the social outcast, the acquirements and skill of the intemperate or over-competed tradesman, all were welcome to the Maryland tobacco-planters ; and the possibilities of rehabilitation of fortune, health, reputation, or reëstablishment of rectitude, made the custom not unwelcome to the convict or to the redemptioner. Were the undoubted servant no rogue, but an honest tradesman, crimped in English coast-towns and haled off to Chesapeake tobacco fields, he did not travel or sojourn, perforce, in low company. He might find himself in as choice companionship, with ladies and gentlemen of as high quality, albeit of the same character, as graced those other English harbors of ne'er-do-weels, Newgate or the Fleet Prison. Convicts came to other colonies, but not so openly nor with so much welcome as to Maryland.

All the convicts who came to the colonies were not rogues, though they might be condemned persons. The first record in Talbot County, Maryland, of the sale of a convict, was in September, 1716, "in the third Yeare of the Reign of our Sovereign Lord King George." And it was for rebellion and treason against his Majesty that this convict, Alexander MacQueen, was taken in Lancashire and transported to America, and sold to Mr. Daniel Sherwood for seven years of service. With him were transported two shiploads of fellow-culprits, Jacobites, on the Friendship and Goodspeed. The London Public Record Office (on American and West India matters, No. 27) records this transportation and says the men were "Scotts Rebells." Earlier still, many of the rebels of Monmouth's rebellion had been sold for transportation, and the ladies of the court of James had eagerly snatched at the profits of the sale. Even William Penn begged for twenty of these rebels for the Philadelphia market. Perhaps he was shrewd enough to see in them good stock for successful citizens. Were the convict a condemned criminal, it did not necessarily follow that he or she was thoroughly vicious. One English husband is found petitioning on behalf of his wife, sentenced to death for stealing but three shillings and sixpence, that her sentence be changed to transportation to Virginia.

The redemptioners were willing immigrants, who contracted to serve for a period of time to pay the cost of their passage, which usually had been prepaid to the master of the ship on which they came across-seas. At first the state of these free-willers was not unbearable. Alsop, who was a redemptioner, has left on record that the work required was not excessive : —

Five dayes and a halfe in the summer is the allotted time that they worke, and for two months, when the Sun is predominate in the highest pitch of his heat, they claim an antient and customary

Priviledge to repose themselves three hours in the day within the house. In Winter they do little but hunt and build fires.

and he adds, "the four years I served there were not to me so slavish as a two-year's servitude of a handicraft apprenticeship in London."

Many examples can be given where these redemptioners rose to respected social positions. In 1654, in the Virginia Assembly were two members and one Burgess who had been bond-servants. Many women-servants married into the family of their employers. Alsop said it was the rule for them to marry well. The niece of Daniel Defoe ran away to escape a marriage entanglement in England, sold herself on board ship as a redemptioner when but eighteen years old, was bought by a Mr. Job of Cecil County, Maryland, and soon married her employer's son. Defoe himself said that so many good maid-servants were sold to America that there was a lack for domestic service in England.

Through the stealing of children and youths to sell in the plantations, it can plainly be seen that many a wife of respectable birth was furnished to the colonists.

This trade, by which, as Lionel Gatford wrote in 1657, young people were "cheatingly duckoyed by Poestigeous Plagiaries," grew to a vast extent, and in it, emulating the noble ladies of the court, women of lower rank sought a degrading profit.

In 1655, in Middlesex, England, one Christian Sacrett was called to answer the complaint of Dorothy Perkins : —

She accuseth her for a spirit, one that takes upp men women and children, and sells them a-shipp to be conveyed beyond the sea, having inticed and inveigled one Edward Furnifall and Anna his wife with her infant to the waterside, and putt them aboard the ship called the Planter to be conveied to Virginia.

Sarah Sharp was also asserted to be a "common taker of children and setter to Betray young men and maydens to be conveyed to ships."

The life of that famous rogue, Bamfylde-Moore Carew, shows the method by which servants were sold in the plantations. The captain, with his cargo of trapanned Englishmen, among whom was Carew, cast anchor at Miles River in Talbot County, Maryland, ordered a gun to be fired, and a hogshead of rum sent on board. On the day of the sale the men prisoners were all shaved, the women dressed in their best garments, their neatest caps, and brought on deck. Each prisoner, when put up for sale, told his trade. Carew said he was a good rat-catcher, beggar, and dog-trader, "upon which the Captain hearing takes the planter aside, and tells him he did but jest, being a man of humour, and would make an excellent school-master." Carew escaped before being sold, was captured, whipped, and had a heavy iron collar, "called in Maryland a pot-hook," riveted about his neck; but he again fled to the Indians, and returned to England. Kidnapped in Bristol a second time, he was nearly sold on Kent Island to Mr. Dulaney, but again escaped. He stole from a house "jolly cake, powell, a sort of Indian corn bread, and good omani, which is kidney beans ground with Indian corn, sifted, put into a pot to boil, and eaten with molasses." Jolly cake was doubtless johnny cake; omani, hominy; but powell is a puzzle. He made his way by begging to Boston, and shipped to England, from whence he was again tra-panned.

In the *Sot-Weed Factor* are found some very coarse but graphic pictures of the women emigrants of the day. When the factor asks the name of " one who passed for chambermaid" in one planter's house in "Mary-Land," she answered with an affected blush and simper : —

> In better Times, ere to this Land
> I was unhappily Trapanned,
> Perchance as well I did appear
> As any lord or lady here.
> Not then a slave for twice two year.
> My cloaths were fashionably new,
> Nor were my shifts of Linnen blue ;
> But things are changed, now at the Hoe
> I daily work, and barefoot go.
> In weeding corn, or feeding swine,
> I spend my melancholy time.
> Kidnap'd and fool'd I hither fled,
> To shun a hated nuptial Bed.
> And to my cost already find
> Worse Plagues than those I left behind.

Another time, being disturbed in his sleep, the factor finds that in an adjoining room, —

> . . . a jolly Female Crew
> Were Deep engaged in Lanctie Loo.

Soon quarreling over their cards, the planters' wives fall into abuse, and one says scornfully to the other : —

> . . . tho now so brave,
> I knew you late a Four Years Slave,
> What if for planters wife you go,
> Nature designed you for the Hoe.

The other makes, in turn, still more bitter accusations. It can plainly be seen that such social and domestic relations might readily produce similar scenes, and afford opportunity for "crimination and recrimination."

Still we must not give the *Sot-Weed Factor* as sole or indeed as entirely unbiased authority. The testimony to the housewifely virtues of the Maryland women by other writers is almost universal. In the *London Magazine* of 1745 a traveler writes, and his word is similar to that of many others : —

The women are very handsome in general and most notable housewives; everything wears the Marks of Cleanliness and Industry in their Houses, and their behavior to their Husbands and Families is very edifying. You cant help observing, however, an Air of Reserve and somewhat that looks at first to a Stranger like Unsociableness, which is barely the effect of living at a great Distance from frequent Society and their Thorough Attention to the Duties of their Stations. Their Amusements are quite Innocent and within the Circle of a Plantation or two. They exercise all the Virtues that can raise Ones Opinion of too light a Sex.

The girls under such good Mothers generally have twice the Sense and Discretion of the Boys. Their Dress is neat and Clean and not much bordering upon the Ridiculous Humour of the Mother Country where the Daughters seem Dress'd up for a Market.

Wives were just as eagerly desired in New England as in Virginia, and a married estate was just as essential to a man of dignity. As a rule, emigration thereto was in families, but when New England men came to the New World, leaving their families behind them until they had prepared a suitable home for their reception, the husbands were most impatient to send speedily for their consorts. Letters such as this, of Mr. Eyre from England to Mr. Gibb in Piscataquay, in 1631, show the sentiment of the settlers in the matter : —

I hope by this both your wives are with you according to your desire. I wish all your wives were with you, and that so many of you as desire wives had such as they desire. Your wife, Roger

Knight's wife, and one wife more we have already sent you and more you shall have as you wish for them.

This sentence, though apparently polygamous in sentiment, does not indicate an intent to establish a Mormon settlement in New Hampshire, but is simply somewhat shaky in grammatical construction, and erratic in rhetorical expression.

Occasionally, though rarely, there was found a wife who did not long for a New England home. Governor Winthrop wrote to England on July 4, 1632 : —

I have much difficultye to keepe John Gallope heere by reason his wife will not come. I marvayle at her womans weaknesse, that she will live myserably with her children there when she might live comfortably with her husband here. I pray perswade and further her coming by all means. If she will come let her have the remainder of his wages, if not let it be bestowed to bring over his children for soe he desires.

Even the ministers' wives did not all sigh for the New World. The removal of Rev. Mr. Wilson to New England " was rendered difficult by the indisposition of his dearest

consort thereto." He very shrewdly interpreted a dream to her in favor of emigration,
with but scant and fleeting influence upon
her, and he sent over to her from America
encouraging accounts of the new home, and
he finally returned to England for her, and
after much fasting and prayer she consented
to "accompany him over an ocean to a
wilderness."

Margaret Winthrop, that undaunted yet
gentle woman, wrote of her at this date (and
it gives us a glimpse of a latent element of
Madam Winthrop's character), "Mr. Wilson
cannot yet persuade his wife to go, for all he
hath taken this pains to come and fetch her.
I marvel what mettle she is made of. Sure
she will yield at last." She did yield, and
she did not go uncomforted. Cotton Mather
wrote : —

Mrs. Wilson being thus perswaded over into
the difficulties of an American desart, her kinsman Old Mr. Dod, for her consolation under
those difficulties did send her a present with an
advice which had in it something of curiosity.
He sent her a *brass* counter, a *silver* crown, and
a *gold* jacobus, all severally wrapped up ; with
this instruction unto the gentleman who carried

it; that he should first of all deliver only the counter, and if she received it with any shew of discontent, he should then take no notice of her; but if she gratefully resented that small thing for the sake of the hand it came from, he should then go on to deliver the silver and so the gold, but withal assure her that such would be the dispensations to her and the good people of New England. If they would be content and thankful with such little things as God at first bestowed upon them, they should, in time, have silver and gold enough. Mrs. Wilson accordingly by her cheerful entertainment of the least remembrance from good old Mr. Dod, gave the gentleman occasion to go through with his whole present and the annexed advice.

We could not feel surprised if poor homesick, heartsick, terrified Mrs. Wilson had "gratefully resented" Mr. Dod's apparently mean gift to her on the eve of exile in our modern sense of resentment; but the meaning of resent in those days was to perceive with a lively sense of pleasure. I do not know whether this old Mr. Dod was the poet whose book entitled *A Posie from Old Mr. Dods Garden* was one of the first rare books of poetry printed in New England in colonial days.

We truly cannot from our point of view " marvayle" that these consorts did not long to come to the strange, sad, foreign shore, but wonder that they were any of them ever willing to come ; for to the loneliness of an unknown world was added the dread horror of encounter with a new and almost mysterious race, the blood-thirsty Indians, and if the poor dames turned from the woods to the shore, they were menaced by " murthering pyrates."

Gurdon Saltonstall, in a letter to John Winthrop of Connecticut, as late as 1690, tells in a few spirited and racy sentences of the life the women lead in an unprotected coast town. It was sad and terrifying in reality, but there is a certain quaintness of expression and metaphor in the narrative, and a sly and demure thrusting at Mr. James, that give it an element of humor. It was written of the approach of a foe " whose entrance was as formidable and swaggering as their exit was sneaking and shamefull." Saltonstall says : —

My Wife & family was posted at your Hon[rs] a considerable while, it being thought to be ye most convenient place for ye feminine Rendezvous. Mr James who Commands in Chiefe among them, upon ye coast alarum given, faceth to ye Mill, gathers like a Snow ball as he goes, makes a Generall Muster at yor Hon^rs, and so posts away with ye greatest speed, to take advantage of ye neighboring rocky hills, craggy, inaccessible mountains; so that W^tever els is lost Mr James and ye Women are safe.

All women did not run at the approach of the foe. A marked trait of the settlers' wives was their courage; and, indeed, opportunities were plentiful for them to show their daring, their fortitude, and their ready ingenuity. Hannah Bradley, of Haverhill, Mass., killed one Indian by throwing boiling soap upon him. This same domestic weapon was also used by some Swedish women near Philadelphia to telling, indeed to killing advantage. A young girl in the Minot House in Dorchester, Mass., shovelled live coals on an Indian invader, and drove him off. A girl, almost a child, in Maine, shut a door, barred, and held it while thirteen women and children escaped to a neighboring blockhouse before the door and its brave defender were chopped down. Anthony Bracket and his wife, captured by savages, escaped through

the wife's skill with the needle. She literally sewed together a broken birch-bark canoe
which they found, and in which they got
safely away. Most famous and fierce of all
women fighters was Hannah Dustin, who, in
1697, with another woman and a boy, killed
ten Indians at midnight, and started for
home; but, calling to mind a thought that
no one at home, without corroborative evidence, would believe this extraordinary tale,
they returned, scalped their victims, and
brought home the bloody trophies safely to
Haverhill.

Some Englishwomen were forced to marry
their captors, forced by torture or dire distress. Some, when captured in childhood,
learned to love their savage husbands.
Eunice Williams, daughter of the Deerfield
minister, a Puritan who hated the Indians
and the church of Rome worse than he hated
Satan, came home to her Puritan kinsfolk
wearing two abhorred symbols, a blanket
and crucifix, and after a short visit, not lik-
ing a civilized life, returned to her Indian
brave, her wigwam, and her priest.

I have always been glad that it was my
far-away grandfather, John Hoar, who left

his Concord home, and risked his life as ambassador to the Indians to rescue one of these poor "captivated" English wives, Mrs. Mary Rowlandson, after her many and heart-rending "savage removes." I am proud of his "very forward spirit" which made him dare attempt this bold rescue, as I am proud of his humanity and his intelligent desire to treat the red men as human beings, furnishing about sixty of them with a home and decent civilizing employment. I picture him "stoutly not afraid," as he entered the camp, and met the poor captive, and treated successfully with her savage and avaricious master, and then I see him tenderly leading her, ragged, half-starved, and exhausted, through the lonely forests home — home to the "doleful solemn sight" of despoiled Lancaster. And I am proud, too, of the noble "Boston gentlewomen" who raised twenty pounds as a ransom for Mary Rowlandson, "the price of her redemption," and tenderly welcomed her to their homes and hearts, so warmly that she could write of them as "pitiful, tender-hearted, and compassionate Christians," whose love was so bountiful that she could not declare it. If any one to-day marvels that English wives did not "much desire the new and doleful land," let them read this graphic and thrilling story of the *Captivity, Removes, and Restauration of Mary Rowlandson,* and he will marvel that the ships were not crowded with disheartened settlers returning to their "faire English homes."

A very exciting and singular experience befell four dignified Virginian wives in Bacon's Rebellion, not through the Indians but at the hands of their erstwhile friends. It is evident that the women of that colony were universally and deeply stirred by the romance of this insurrection and war. We hear of their dramatic protests against the tyranny of the government. Sarah Drummond ·vowed she feared the power of England no more than a broken straw, and contemptuously broke a stick of wood to illustrate her words. Major Chriesman's wife, "the honor of her sex," when her husband was about to be put to death as a rebel, begged Governor Berkeley to kill her instead, as he had joined Bacon wholly at her solicitation. One Ann Cotton was moved by the war to drop into literary composition, an extraordinary ebullition for a woman in her day, and to write an account of the Rebellion, as she deemed "too wordishly," but which does not read now very wordishly to us. But for these four dames, the wives of men prominent in the army under Governor Berkeley — prime men, Ann Cotton calls them — was decreed a more stirring participation in the excitements of war. The brilliant and erratic young rebel, Bacon, pressed them into active service. He sent out companies of horsemen and tore the gentlewomen from their homes, though they remonstrated with much simplicity that they were "indisposed" to leave; and he brought them to the scene of battle, and heartlessly placed them — with still further and more acute indisposition — on the "fore-front" of the breastworks as a shield against the attacks of the four distracted husbands with their soldiers. We read that "the poor Gentlewomen were mightily astonished at this project; neather were their husbands void of amazements at this subtill invention." The four dames were "exhibited to the view of their husbands and ffriends in the towne upon the top of the smalle worke he had cast up in the night where he caused them to tarey till he had finished his defence against the enemy's shott." There stood these four innocent and harmless wives, — "guardian angells — the white gardes of the Divell," shivering through the chill September night till the glimmering dawn saw completed the rampart of earth and logs, or the leaguer, as it was called by the writers with that exactness and absolute fitness of expression which, in these old chronicles, gives such delight to the lover of good old English. One dame was also sent to her husband's camp as a "white-aproned hostage" to parley with the Governor. And this hiding of soldiers behind women was done by the order of one who was called the most accomplished gentleman in Virginia, but whom we might dub otherwise if we wished, to quote the contemporary account, to "oppose him further with pertinances and violent perstringes."

I wish I could truthfully say that one most odious and degrading eighteenth century English custom was wholly unknown in America — the custom of wife-trading, the selling by a husband of his wife to another

man. I found, for a long time, no traces or
hints of the existence of such a custom in
the colonies, save in two doubtful cases. I
did not wholly like the aspect of Governor
Winthrop's note of the suggestion of some
members of the church in Providence, that
if Goodman Verin would not give his wife
full liberty to go to meeting on Sunday
and weekly lectures as often as she wished,
"the church should dispose her to some
other man who would use her better." I
regarded this suggestion of the Providence
Christians with shocked suspicion, but calmed
myself with the decision that it merely indi-
cated the disposition of Goodwife Verin as
a servant. And again, in the records of the
"Pticuler Court" of Hartford, Conn., in
1645, I discovered this entry: "Baggett
Egleston for bequething his wyfe to a young
man is fyned 20 shillings." Now, any reader
can draw his conclusions as to exactly what
this "bequething" was, and I cannot see that
any of us can know positively. So, though
I was aware that Baggett was not a very re
putable fellow, I chose to try to persuade
myself that this exceedingly low-priced be-
queathing did not really mean wife-selling.

But just as I was "setting down satysfyed" at the superiority in social ethics and morality of our New England ancestors, I chanced, while searching in the *Boston Evening Post* of March 15, 1736, for the advertisement of a sermon on the virtues of our forbears, entitled *New England Tears and Fears of Englands Dolours and Horrours*, to find instead, by a malicious and contrary fate, this bit of unwelcome and mortifying news not about old England but about New England's "dolours and horrours."

Boston. The beginning of last Week a pretty odd and uncommon Adventure happened in this Town, between 2 Men about a certain woman, each one claiming her as his Wife, but so it was, that one of them had actually disposed of his Right in her to the other for Fifteen Shillings this Currency, who had only paid ten of it in part, and refus'd to pay the other Five, inclining rather to quit the Woman and lose his Earnest; but two Gentlemen happening to be present, who were Friends to Peace, charitably gave him half a Crown a piece, to enable him to fulfil his Agreement, which the Creditor readily took, and gave the Woman a modest Salute, wishing her well, and his Brother Sterling much Joy of his Bargain.

The meagre sale-money, fifteen shillings, was the usual sum which changed hands in England at similar transactions, though one dame of high degree was sold for a hundred guineas. In 1858 the *Stamford Mercury* gave an account of a contemporary wife-sale in England, which was announced through the town by a bellman. The wife was led to the sale with a halter round her neck, and was "to be taken with all her faults." I am glad to say that this base British husband was sharply punished for his misdemeanor.

It seems scarcely credible that the custom still exists in England, but in 1882 a husband sold his wife in Alfreton, Derbyshire; and as late as the 13th July, 1887, Abraham Boothroyd, may his name be *Anathema maranatha*, sold his wife Clara at Sheffield, England, for five shillings.

A most marked feature of social life in colonial times was the belleship of widows. They were literally the queens of society. Fair maids had so little chance against them, swains were so plentiful for widows, that I often wonder whence came the willing men who married the girls the first time, thus offering themselves as the sacrifice at the matrimonial altar through which the girls could attain the exalted state of widowhood. Men sighed sometimes in their callow days for the girl friends of their own age, but as soon as their regards were cast upon a widow, the girls at once disappear from history, and the triumphant widow wins the prize.

Another marked aspect of this condition of society was the vast number of widows in early days. In the South this was accounted for by one of their own historians as being through the universally intemperate habits of the husbands, and consequently their frequent early death. In all the colonies life was hard, exposure was great to carry on any active business, and the excessive drinking of intoxicating liquors was not peculiar to the Southern husbands any more than were widows. In 1698 Boston was said to be "full of widows and orphans, and many of them very helpless creatures." It was counted that one sixth of the communicants of Cotton Mather's church were widows. It is easy for us to believe this when we read of the array of relicts among which that aged but actively amorous gentleman, Judge Sewall, found so much difficulty in choosing a marriage partner, whose personal and financial charms he recounted with so much pleasurable minuteness in his diary.

A glowing tribute to one of these Boston widows was paid by that gossiping traveller, John Dunton, with so much evidence of deep interest, and even sentiment, that I fancy Madam Dunton could not have been wholly pleased with the writing and the printing thereof. He called this Widow Breck the "flower of Boston," the "Chosen exemplar of what a Widow is." He extols her high character, beauty, and resignation, and then bridles with satisfaction while he says, "Some have been pleas'd to say That were I in a single state they do believe she wou'd not be displeas'd with my addresses." He rode on horseback on a long journey with his fair widow on a pillion behind him, and if his conversation on "Platonicks and the blisses of Matrimony" was half as tedious as his recounting of it, the road must indeed have seemed long. He says her love for her dead husband is as strong as death, but Widow Breck proved the strength of her constancy by speedily marrying a second husband, Michael Perry.

As an instance of the complicated family relations which might arise in marrying widows, let me cite the familiar case of the rich merchant, Peter Sergeant, the builder of the famous Province House in Boston. I will use Mr. Shurtleff's explanation of this bewildering gallimaufrey of widows and widowers : —

He was as remarkable in his marriages as his wealth ; for he had three wives, the second having been a widow twice before her third venture ; and his third also a widow, and even becoming his widow, and lastly the widow of her third husband.

To this I may add that this last husband, Simon Stoddart, also had three wives, that his father had four, of whom the last three were widows, — but all this goes beyond the modern brain to comprehend, and reminds us most unpleasantly of the wife of Bath.

These frequent and speedy marriages were not wholly owing to the exigencies of colonial life, but were the custom of the times in Europe as well. I read in the diary of the Puritan John Rous, in January, 1638, of this somewhat hasty wooing : —

A gentleman carried his wife to London last

week and died about eight o'clock at night, leaving her five hundred pounds a year in land. The next day before twelve she was married to the journeyman woolen-draper that came to sell mourning to her.

I do not believe John Rous made special note of this marriage simply because it was so speedy, but because it was unsuitable ; as a landed widow was, in social standing, far above a journeyman draper.

As we approach Revolutionary days, the reign of widows is still absolute.

Washington loved at fifteen a fair unknown, supposed to be Lucy Grimes, afterward mother of Gen. Henry Lee. To her he wrote sentimental poems, from which we gather (as might be expected at that age) that he was too bashful to reveal his love. A year later he writes : —

I might, was my heart disengaged, pass my time very pleasantly as there 's a very agreeable Young Lady Lives in the same house; but as thats only adding fuel to the fire it makes me more uneasy; for by often and unavoidably being in Company with her revives my former Passion for your Lowland Beauty; whereas was I to live more retired from young women, I might in some measure eliviate my sorrows by burying that chast and troublesome passion in the grave of oblivion or eternal forgetfulness.

The amorous boy of sixteen managed to "bury this chast and troublesome passion," to find the "Young Lady in the house" worth looking at, and when he was twenty years old, to write to William Fantleroy thus of his daughter, Miss Bettie Fantleroy : —

I purpose as soon as I recover my strength (from the pleurisy) to wait on Miss Bettie in hopes of a reconsideration of the former cruel sentence, and to see if I cannot obtain a decision in my favor. I enclose a letter to her.

Later he fell in love with Mary Phillipse, who, though beautiful, spirited, and rich, did not win him. This love affair is somewhat shadowy in outline. Washington Irving thinks that the spirit of the alert soldier overcame the passion of the lover, and that Washington left the lists of love for those of battle, leaving the field to his successful rival, Colonel Morris. The inevitable widow in the shape of Madam Custis, with two pretty children and a fortune of fifteen thousand pounds sterling, became at last what he called his "agreeable partner for life," and Irving thinks she was wooed with much despatch on account of the reverses in the Phillipse episode.

Thomas Jefferson was another example of a President who outlived his love-affair with a young girl, and married in serenity a more experienced dame. In his early correspondence he reveals his really tumultuous passion for one Miss Becca Burwell. He sighs like a furnace, and bemoans his stammering words of love, but fair Widow Martha Skelton made him eloquent. Many lovers sighed at her feet; two of them lingered in her drawing-room one evening to hear her sing a thrilling love-song to the accompaniment of Jefferson's violin. The love-song and music were so expressive that the two disconsolate swains plainly read the story of their fate, and left the house in defeat.

James Madison, supposed to be an irreclaimable old bachelor, succumbed at first sight to the charms of fair Widow Dorothy Todd, twenty years his junior, wooed her with warmth, and made her, as Dolly Madison, another Mrs. President. Benjamin Franklin also married a widow.

The characteristic glamour which hung round every widow encircled Widow Sarah Syms, and Colonel Byrd gives a spirited sketch of her in 1732 : —

In the evening Tinsley conducted me to Widow Syms' house where I intended to take up my quarters. This lady at first suspecting I was some lover put on a gravity that becomes a weed, but as soon as she learned who I was brightened up with an unusual cheerfulness and serenity. She was a portly handsome dame, of the family of Esau, and seemed not to pine too much for the death of her husband. This widow is a person of lively and cheerful conversation with much less reserve than most of her country women. It becomes her very well and sets off her other agreeable qualities to advantage. We tossed off a bottle of honest port which we relished with a broiled chicken. At nine I retired to my devotions, and then slept so sound that fancy itself was stupefied, else I should have dreamed of my most obliging landlady.

This "weed" who did not pine too much for her husband, soon married again, and became the mother of Patrick Henry ; and the testimony of Colonel Byrd as to her lively and cheerful conversation shows the heredity of Patrick Henry's "gift of tongues."

> Hie! Betty Martin! tiptoe fine,
> Could n't get a husband for to suit her mind!

was a famous Maryland belle, to whom came a-courting two friends, young lawyers, named Dallam and Winston. It was a day of much masculine finery and the two impecunious but amicable friends possessed but one ruffled shirt between them, which each wore on courting-day. Such amiability deserved the reward it obtained, for, strange to say, both suitors won Betty Martin. Dallam was the first husband, — the sacrifice, — and left her a widow with three sons and a daughter. Winston did likewise, even to the exact number of children. Daughter Dallam's son was Richard Caswell, governor of South Carolina, and member of Congress. Daughter Winston's son was William Paca, governor of Maryland, and member of the Continental Congress. Both grandsons on their way to and from Congress always visited their spirited old grandmother, who lived to be some say one hundred and twenty years old.

There must have been afforded a certain satisfaction to a dying husband — of colonial times — through the confidence that, by unwavering rule, his widow would soon be cared for and cherished by another. There was no uncertainty as to her ultimate settlement in life, and even should she be unfortunate enough to lose her second partner, he still had every reason to believe that a third would speedily present himself. The Reverend Jonathan Burr when almost moribund, piously expressed himself to "that vertuous gentlewoman his wife with confidence" that she would soon be well provided for; and she was, for "she was very shortly after very honourably and comfortably married unto a gentleman of good estate," a magistrate, Richard Dummer, and lived with him nearly forty years. Provisions were always made by a man in his will in case his wife married again; scarcely ever to remove the property from her, but simply to re-adjust the division or conditions. And men often signed ante-nuptial contracts promising not to "meddle" with their wives' property. One curious law should be noted in Pennsylvania, in 1690, that a widow could not marry till a year after her husband's death.

There seem to have been many advantages in marrying a widow — she might prove a valuable inheritance. The second husband appeared to take a real pride in demanding and receiving all that was due to the defunct partner. As an example let me give this extract from a court record. On May 31st, 1692, the governor and council of Maryland were thus petitioned : —

James Brown of St Marys who married the widow and relict of Thomas Pew deceased, by his petition humbly prays allowance for Two Years Sallary due to his Predecessor as Publick Post employed by the Courts, as also for the use of a Horse, and the loss of a Servant wholly, by the said Pew deputed in his sickness to Officiate ; and ran clear away with his Horse, some Clothes &c., and for several months after not heard of.

Now we must not be over-critical, nor hasty in judgment of the manners and motives of two centuries ago, but those days are held up to us as days of vast submissiveness and modesty, of patient long-suffering, of ignorance of extortion; yet I think we would search far, in these degenerate days, for a man who, having married a relict, would, two years after his "Predecessor's" death, have the colossal effrontery to demand of the government not only the back salary of said "Predecessor," but pay for the use of a horse stolen by the Predecessor's own servant — nay, more, for the value of the said servant who elected to run away. Truly James Brown builded well when he chose a wife whose departing partner had, like a receding wave, deposited much lucrative silt on the matrimonial shore, to be thriftily gathered in and utilized as a bridal dower by his not-too-sensitive successor.

In fact it may plainly be seen that widows were life-saving stations in colonial social economy; one colonist expressed his attitude towards widows and their Providential function as economic aids, thus : —

Our uncle is not at present able to pay you or any other he owes money to. If he was able to pay he would; they must have patience till God enable him. As his wife died in mercy near twelve months since, it may be he may light of some rich widow that may make him capable

to pay ; except God in this way raise him he cannot pay you or any one else.

It certainly must have been some satisfaction to every woman to feel within herself
the possibility of becoming such a celestial
agent of material salvation.

I wish to state, in passing, that it is sometimes difficult to judge as to the marital
estate of some dames, to know whether they
were widows at the time of the second marriage or not, for the prefixed Mrs. was used
indifferently for married and single women,
and even for young girls. Cotton Mather
wrote of " Mrs. Sarah Gerrish, a very beautiful and ingenious damsel seven years of
age." Rev. Mr. Tompson wrote a funeral
tribute to a little girl of six, which is entitled
and begins thus : —

A Neighbors Tears dropt on ye grave of an
Amiable Virgin, a pleasant Plant cut down in
the blooming of her Spring viz ; Mrs Rebecka
Sewall Anno Aetatis 6, August ye 4th 1710.

> I saw this Pritty Lamb but t' other day
> With a small flock of Doves just in my way
> Ah pitty tis Such Prittiness should die
> With rare alliances on every side.
> Had Old Physitians liv'd she ne'er had died.

The pious old minister did not really mean
by this tribute to the old-school doctors,
that Mrs. Rebecka would have achieved
earthly immortality. He modestly ends his
poetic tribute thus : —

> Had you given warning ere you pleased to Die
> You might have had a Neater Elegy.

These consorts and relics are now but
shadows of the past : —

> their bones are dust,
> Their souls are with the saints, I trust.

The honest and kindly gentlemen who were
their husbands, sounded their virtues in
diaries and letters ; godly ministers preached
their piety in labored and dry-as-dust ser-
mons. Their charms were sung by colonial
poets in elegies, anagrams, epicediums, acros-
tics, threnodies, and other decorous verse.
It was reserved for a man of war, and not a
very godly man of war either, to pæan their
good sense. Cervantes says that "womans
counsel is not worth much, yet he who de-
spises it is no wiser than he should be."
With John Underhill's more gallant tribute
to the counsel of a consort, we may fitly end
this chapter.

Myself received an arrow through my coat sleeve, a second against my helmet on the forehead; so as if God in his Providence had not moved the heart of my wife to persuade me to carry it along with me (which I was unwilling to do) I had been slain. Give me leave to observe two things from hence; first when the hour of death is not yet come, you see God useth weak means to keep his purpose unviolated; secondly let no man despise advice and counsel of his wife though she be a woman. It were strange to nature to think a man should be bound to fulfil the humour of a woman, what arms he should carry; but you see God will have it so, that a woman should overcome a man. What with Delilahs flattery, and with her mournful tears, they must and will have their desire, when the hand of God goes along in the matter, and this to accomplish his own will. Therefore let the clamor be quenched that I hear daily in my ears, that New England men usurp over their wives and keep them in servile subjection. The country is wronged in this matter as in many things else. Let this precedent satisfy the doubtful, for that comes from the example of a rude soldier. If they be so courteous to their wives as to take their advice in warlike matters, how much more kind is the tender affectionate husband to honor his wife as the weaker vessel.

Yet mistake not. I say not they are bound to
call their wives in council, though they are bound
to take their private advice (so far as they
see it make for their advantage
and good). Instance
Abraham.

CHAPTER II.

THE early history of Maryland seems singularly peaceful when contrasted with that of other colonies. There were few Indian horrors, few bitter quarrels, comparatively few petty offences. In spite of the influx of convicts, there was a notable absence of the shocking crimes and equally shocking punishments which appear on the court records of other provinces; it is also true that there were few schools and churches, and but scanty intellectual activity. Against that comparatively peaceful background stands out one of the most remarkable figures of early colonial life in America — Margaret Brent; a woman who seemed more fitted for our day than her own. She was the first woman in America to demand suffrage, a vote, and representation.

She came to the province in 1638 with her sister Mary (another shrewd and capable woman), her two brothers, and nine other colonists. The sisters at once took up land, built manorhouses, and shortly brought over more colonists; soon the court-baron and court-leet were held at Mary Brent's home, St. Gabriel's Manor, on old Kent Island. We at once hear of the sisters as active in business affairs, registering cattle marks, buying and selling property, attending with success to important matters for their brothers; and Margaret soon signed herself "Attorney for my brother, &c., &c.," and was allowed the right so to act. The Brents were friends and probably kinsfolk of Lord Baltimore, and intimate friends, also, of the governor of Maryland, Leonard Calvert. When the latter died in 1647, he appointed by nuncupation one Thomas Greene as his successor as governor, and Margaret Brent as his sole executrix, with the laconic instruction to "Take all and Pay all," and to give one Mistress Temperance Pypott a mare colt. His estate was small, and if he had made Greene executor, and Mistress Margaret governor, he would have done a much more sensible thing; for Greene was vacillating and weak, and when an emergency arose, he had to come to Margaret Brent for help. The soldiers, who had assisted the government in recent troubles, were still unpaid, and Governor Calvert had pledged his official word and the property of Lord Baltimore that they should be paid in full. After his death an insurrection in the army seemed rising, when Mistress Brent calmly stepped in, sold cattle belonging to the Proprietary, and paid off the small but angry army. This was not the only time she quelled an incipient mutiny. Her kinsman, Lord Baltimore, was inclined to find bitter fault, and wrote "tartly" when the news of her prompt action and attendant expenditure reached his ears ; but the Assembly sent him a letter, gallantly upholding Mistress Brent in her "meddling," saying with inadvertent humour, that his estate fared better in her hands than "any man elses."

Her astonishing stand for woman's rights was made on January 21, 1647–48, two centuries and a half ago, and was thus recorded : —

Came Mrs Margaret Brent and requested to have vote in the House for herself and voyce allsoe, for that on the last Court 3rd January it

was ordered that the said Mrs Brent was to be
looked upon and received as his Ldp's Attorney.
The Governor deny'd that the s'd Mrs Brent
should have any vote in the house.   And the s'd
Mrs Brent protested against all proceedings in
this present Assembly unlesse she may be present
and have vote as afores'd.

With this protest for representation, and
demand for her full rights, this remarkable
woman does not disappear from our ken.
We hear of her in 1651 as an offender, having been accused of killing wild cattle and
selling the beef.   She asserted with vigor
and dignity that the cattle were her own, and
demanded a trial by jury.

And in 1658 she makes her last curtsey
before the Assembly and ourselves, a living
proof of the fallacy of the statement that
men do not like strong-minded women.   For
at that date, at the fully ripened age of fifty-
seven, she appeared as heir of an estate bequeathed to her by a Maryland gentleman as
a token of his love and affection, and of his
constant wish to marry her.   She thus vanishes out of history, in a thoroughly emin-
ine rôle, that of a mourning sweetheart ; yet
standing signally out of colonial days as the

most clear-cut, unusual, and forceful figure of the seventeenth century in Maryland.

Another Maryland woman of force and fearlessness was Verlinda Stone. A letter from her to Lord Baltimore is still in the Maryland archives, demanding an investigation of a fight in Anne Arundel County, in which her husband was wounded. The letter is businesslike enough, but ends in a fiery postscript in which she uses some pretty strong terms. Such women as these were not to be trifled with ; as Alsop wrote : —

All Complemental Courtships drest up in critical Rarities are meer Strangers to them. Plain wit comes nearest to their Genius, so that he that intends to Court a Maryland girle, must have something more than the tautologies of a long-winded speech to carry on his design.

Elizabeth Haddon was another remarkable woman ; she founded Haddonfield, New Jersey. Her father had become possessed of a tract of land in the New World, and she volunteered to come alone to the colony, and settle upon the land. She did so in 1701 when she was but *nineteen years old*, and conducted herself and her business with

judgment, discretion, and success, and so
continued throughout her long life. She
married a young Quaker named Esthaugh,
who may have been one of the attractions of
the New World. Her idealized story has
been told by L. Maria Child in her book
The Youthful Emigrant.

John Clayton, writing as early as 1688 of
"Observables" in Virginia, tells of several
"acute ingenious gentlewomen" who carried
on thriving tobacco-plantations, draining
swamps and raising cattle and buying slaves.
One near Jamestown was a fig-raiser.

In all the Southern colonies we find these
acute gentlewomen taking up tracts of land,
clearing them, and cultivating their hold-
ings. In the settlement of Pennsylvania,
Mary Tewee took two thousand five hundred
acres in what is now Lancaster County. She
was the widow of a French Huguenot gentleman, the friend of William Penn, and had
been presented at the court of Queen Anne.

New England magistrates did not encourage such independence. In the early days
of Salem, "maid-lotts" were granted to single women, but stern Endicott wrote that it
was best to abandon the custom, and "avoid

all presedents & evil events of granting lotts vnto single maidens not disposed of." The town of Taunton, Mass., had an "ancient maid" of forty-eight years for its founder, one Elizabeth Poole; and Winthrop says she endured much hardship. Her gravestone says she was a "native of old England of good family, friends and prospects, all of which she left in the prime of her life to enjoy the religion of her conscience in this distant wilderness. A great proprietor of the township of Taunton, a chief promoter of its settlement in 1639. Having employed the opportunity of her virgin state in piety, liberality and sanctity of manners, she died aged 65."

Lady Deborah Moody did not receive from the Massachusetts magistrates an over-cordial or very long-lived welcome. She is described as a "harassed and lonely widow voluntarily exiling herself for conscience' sake." Perhaps her running in debt for her Swampscott land and her cattle had quite as much to do with her unpopularity as her "error of denying infant baptism." But as she paid nine hundred or some say eleven hundred pounds for that wild land, it is no wonder she was

83805

"almost undone." She was dealt with by the elders, and admonished by the church, but she "persisted" and finally removed to the Dutch, against the advice of all her friends. Endicott called her a dangerous woman, but Winthrop termed her a "wise and anciently religious woman." Among the Dutch she found a congenial home, and, unmolested, she planned on her Gravesend farm a well-laid-out city, but did not live to carry out her project. A descendant of one of her Dutch neighbors writes of her : —

Tradition says she was buried in the northwest corner of the Gravesend church yard. Upon the headstone of those who sleep beside her we read the inscription *In der Heere entslapen* — they sleep in the Lord. We may say the same of this brave true woman, she sleeps in the Lord. Her rest has been undisturbed in this quiet spot which she hoped to make a great city.

It seems to be plain that the charge of the affairs of Governor John Winthrop, Jr., in New Haven was wholly in the hands of Mrs. Davenport, the wife of the minister, Rev. John Davenport. Many sentences in her husband's letters show her cares for her friends' welfare, the variety of her business

duties, and her performance of them. He
wrote thus to the Governor in 1658 : —

For your ground; my wife speedily, even the
same day she received your letter, spake with
sundry about it, and received this answer, that
there is no Indian corne to be planted in that
quarter this yeare. Brother Boykin was willing
to have taken it, but saith it is overrun with wild
sorrell and it will require time to subdue it, and
put it into tillage, being at present unfit to be improved. Goodman Finch was in our harbour
when your letter came, & my wife went promptly
downe, and met with yong Mr Lamberton to
whom she delivered your letter. He offered
some so bad beaver that my wife would not take
it. My wife spake twise to him herself. My
wife desireth to add that she received for you of
Mr Goodenhouse 30s worth of beaver & 4s in
wampum. She purposeth to send your beaver to
the Baye when the best time is, to sell it for your
advantage and afterwards to give you an account
what it comes to. Your letter to Sarjiunt Bald-
win my wife purposeth to carry to him by the 1st
opportunity. Sister Hobbadge has paid my wife
in part of her debt to you a bushel of winter
wheate.

The letters also reveal much loving-kind-
ness, much eagerness to be of assistance,

equal readiness to welcome new-comers, and
to smooth the rough difficulties in pioneer
housekeeping. Rev. Mr. Davenport wrote
in August, 1655, from New Haven to Gov.
Winthrop at Pequot : —

HON'ᴰ SIR, — We did earnestly expect your
coming hither with Mrs. Winthrop and your fam-
ilie, the last light moone, having intelligence
that a vessel wayted upon you at Pequot for that
end, and were thereby encouraged to provide
your house, that it might be fitted in some
measure, for your comfortable dwelling in it,
this winter.

My wife was not wanting in her endeavors
to set all wheeles in going, all hands that she
could procure on worke, that you might find all
things to your satisfaction. Though she could
not accomplish her desires to the full, yet she
proceeded as farr as she could ; whereby many
things are done viz. the house made warme, the
well cleansed, the pumpe fitted for your use, some
provision of wood layed in, and 20 loades will be
ready, whensoever you come ; and sundry, by my
wife's instigation, prepared 30 bush. of wheate for
the present and sister Glover hath 12 lb of candles ready for you. My wife hath also procured
a maid servant for you, who is reported to be
cleanly and saving, her mother is of the church,

and she is kept from a place in Connectacot where she was much desired, to serve you. . . .

If Mrs. Winthrop knew how wellcome she will be to us she would I believe neglect whatsoever others doe or may be forward to suggest for her discouragement. Salute her, with due respect, in my name and my wife's, most affectionately.

Madam Davenport also furnished the rooms with tables and "chayres," and "took care of yor apples that they may be kept safe from the frost that Mrs. Winthrop may have the benefit of them," and arranged to send horses to meet them; so it is not strange to learn in a postscript that the hospitable kindly soul, who thus cheerfully worked to "redd the house," had a "paine in the soles of her feet, especially in the evening;" and a little later on to know she was "valetudinarious, faint, thirsty, of little appetite *yet cheerful.*"

All these examples, and many others help to correct one very popular mistake. It seems to be universally believed that the "business woman" is wholly a product of the nineteenth century. Most emphatically may it be affirmed that such is not the case. I

have seen advertisements dating from 1720 to
1800, chiefly in New England newspapers, of
women teachers, embroiderers, jelly-makers,
cooks, wax-workers, japanners, mantua-mak-
ers, — all truly feminine employments ; and
also of women dealers in crockery, musical
instruments, hardware, farm products, gro-
ceries, drugs, wines, and spirits, while Haw-
thorne noted one colonial dame who carried
on a blacksmith-shop.   Peter Faneuil's account books show that he had accounts in
small English wares with many Boston
tradeswomen, some of whom bought many
thousand pounds' worth of imported goods
in a year.   Alice Quick had fifteen hundred
pounds in three months ; and I am glad to
say that the women were very prompt in
payment, as well as active in business.   By
Stamp Act times, the names of five women
merchants appear on the Salem list of traders
who banded together to oppose taxation.

It is claimed by many that the "newspaper-woman" is a growth of modern times.
I give examples to prove the fallacy of this
statement.   Newspapers of colonial times
can scarcely be said to have been edited, they
were simply printed or published, and all that

men did as newspaper-publishers, women did also, and did well. It cannot be asserted that these women often voluntarily or primarily started a newspaper; they usually assumed the care after the death of an editor husband, or brother, or son, or sometimes to assist while a male relative, through sickness or multiplicity of affairs, could not attend to his editorial or publishing work.

Perhaps the most remarkable examples of women-publishers may be found in the Goddard family of Rhode Island. Mrs. Sarah Goddard was the daughter of Ludowick Updike, of one of the oldest and most respected families in that State. She received an excellent education "in both useful and polite learning," and married Dr. Giles Goddard, a prominent physician and postmaster of New London. After becoming a widow, she went into the printing business in Providence about the year 1765, with her son, who was postmaster of that town. They published the *Providence Gazette and Country Journal*, the only newspaper printed in Providence before 1775. William Goddard was dissatisfied with his pecuniary profit, and he went to New York, leaving the business wholly with

his mother; she conducted it with much ability and success under the name Sarah Goddard & Company.   I wish to note that she
carried on this business not under her son's
name, but openly in her own behalf; and
when she assumed the charge of the paper,
she printed it with her own motto as the
heading, *Vox Populi Vox Dei.*

William Goddard drifted to Philadelphia,
where he published the *Pennsylvania Chroni-
cle* for a short season, and in 1773 he removed to Baltimore and established himself
in the newspaper business anew, with only,
he relates, "the small capital of a single solitary guinea."   He found another energetic
business woman, the widow Mrs. Nicholas
Hasselbaugh, carrying on the printing-busi-
ness bequeathed to her by her husband;
and he bought her stock in trade and established *The Maryland Journal and Baltimore
Advertiser.*   It was the third newspaper published in Maryland, was issued weekly at ten
shillings per annum, and was a well-printed
sheet.   But William Goddard had another
bee in his bonnet.   A plan was formed just
before the Revolutionary War to abolish the
general public post-office and to establish in

its place a complete private system of post-riders from Georgia to New Hampshire. This system was to be supported by private subscription; a large sum was already subscribed, and the scheme well under way, when the war ended all the plans. Goddard had this much to heart, and had travelled extensively through the colonies exploiting it. While he was away on these trips he left the newspaper and printing-house solely under the charge of his sister Mary Katharine Goddard, the worthy daughter of her energetic mother. From 1775 to 1784, through the trying times of the Revolution, and in a most active scene of military and political troubles, this really brilliant woman continued to print successfully and continuously her newspaper. The *Journal* and every other work issued from her printing-presses were printed and published in her name, and it is believed chiefly on her own account. She was a woman of much intelligence and was also practical, being an expert compositor of types, and fully conversant with every detail of the mechanical work of a printing-office. During this busy time she was also postmistress of Baltimore, and kept a bookshop. Her brother William, through his futile services in this postal scheme, had been led to believe he would receive under Benjamin Franklin and the new government of the United States, the appointment of Secretary and Comptroller of the Post Office; but Franklin gave it to his own son-in-law, Richard Bache. Goddard, sorely disappointed but pressed in money matters, felt forced to accept the position of Surveyor of Post Roads. When Franklin went to France in 1776, and Bache became Postmaster-General, and Goddard again was not appointed Comptroller, his chagrin caused him to resign his office, and naturally to change his political principles.

He retired to Baltimore, and soon there appeared in the *Journal* an ironical piece (written by a member of Congress) signed Tom Tell Truth. From this arose a vast political storm. The Whig Club of Baltimore, a powerful body, came to Miss Goddard and demanded the name of the author; she referred them to her brother. On his refusal to give the author's name, he was seized, carried to the clubhouse, bullied, and finally warned out of town and county. He

at once went to the Assembly at Annapolis
and demanded protection, which was given
him. He ventilated his wrongs in a pam-
phlet, and was again mobbed and insulted.
In 1779, Anna Goddard printed anony-
mously in her paper *Queries Political and
Military*, written really by General Charles
Lee, the enemy and at one time presumptive rival of Washington. This paper also
raised a tremendous storm through which
the Goddards passed triumphantly. Lee
remained always a close friend of William
Goddard, and bequeathed to him his valuable and interesting papers, with the intent
of posthumous publication ; but, unfortu-
nately, they were sent to England to be
printed in handsome style, and were instead
imperfectly and incompletely issued, and
William Goddard received no benefit or
profit from their sale. But Lee left him
also, by will, a large and valuable estate in
Berkeley County, Virginia, so he retired
from public life and ended his days on a
Rhode Island farm. Anna Katharine Goddard lived to great old age. The story of
this acquaintance with General Lee, and of
Miss Goddard's connection therewith, forms

one of the interesting minor episodes of the War.

Just previous to the Revolution, it was nothing very novel or unusual to Baltimoreans to see a woman edit a newspaper. The *Maryland Gazette* suspended on account of the Stamp Act in 1765, and the printer issued a paper called *The Apparition of the Maryland Gazette which is not Dead but Sleepeth;* and instead of a Stamp it bore a death's head with the motto, "The Times are Dismal, Doleful, Dolorous, Dollarless." Almost immediately after it resumed publication, the publisher died, and from 1767 to 1775 it was carried on by his widow, Anne Katharine Green, sometimes assisted by her son, but for five years alone. The firm name was Anne Katharine Green & Son : and she also did the printing for the Colony. She was about thirty-six years old when she assumed the business, and was then the mother of six sons and eight daughters. Her husband was the fourth generation from Samuel Green, the first printer in New England, from whom descended about thirty ante-Revolutionary printers. Until the Revolution there was always a Printer

Green in Boston. Mr. Green's partner, William Rind, removed to Williamsburg and printed there the *Virginia Gazette.* At his death, widow Clementina Rind, not to be outdone by Widow Green and Mother and Sister Goddard, proved that what woman has done woman can do, by carrying on the business and printing the *Gazette* till her own death in 1775.

It is indeed a curious circumstance that, on the eve of the Revolution, so many southern newspapers should be conducted by women. Long ere that, from 1738 to 1740, Elizabeth Timothy, a Charleston woman, widow of Louis Timothy, the first librarian of the Philadelphia Library company, and publisher of the *South Carolina Gazette*, carried on that paper after her husband's death; and her son, Peter Timothy, succeeded her. In 1780 his paper was suspended, through his capture by the British. He was exchanged, and was lost at sea with two daughters and a grandchild, while on his way to Antigua to obtain funds. He had a varied and interesting life, was a friend of Parson Whitefield, and was tried with him on a charge of libel against the South

Carolina ministers. In 1782 his widow, Anne Timothy, revived the *Gazette*, as had her mother-in-law before her, and published it successfully twice a week for ten years till her death in 1792. She had a large printing-house, corner of Broad and King Streets, Charleston, and was printer to the State; truly a remarkable woman.

Peter Timothy's sister Mary married Charles Crouch, who also was drowned when on a vessel bound to New York. He was a sound Whig and set up a paper in opposition to the Stamp Act, called *The South Carolina Gazette and Country Journal.* This was one of the four papers which were all entitled Gazettes in order to secure certain advertisements that were all directed by law "to be inserted in the South Carolina Gazette." Mary Timothy Crouch continued the paper for a short time after her husband's death; and in 1780 shortly before the surrender of the city to the British, went with her printing-press and types to Salem, where for a few months she printed *The Salem Gazette and General Advertiser.* I have dwelt at some length on the activity and enterprise of these Southern women, because it is another popular but unstable notion that the women of the North were far more energetic and capable than their Southern sisters; which is certainly not the case in this line of business affairs.

Benjamin and James Franklin were not the only members of the Franklin family who were capable newspaper-folk. James Franklin died in Newport in 1735, and his widow Anne successfully carried on the business for many years. She had efficient aid in her two daughters, who were quick and capable practical workers at the compositor's case, having been taught by their father, whom they assisted in his lifetime. Isaiah Thomas says of them: —

A gentleman who was acquainted with Anne Franklin and her family, informed me that he had often seen her daughters at work in the printing house, and that they were sensible and amiable women.

We can well believe that, since they had Franklin and Anne Franklin blood in them. This competent and industrious trio of women not only published the *Newport Mercury*, but were printers for the colony, supplying blanks for public offices, publishing pamphlets, etc. In 1745 they printed for the Government an edition of the laws of the colony of 340 pages, folio. Still further, they carried on a business of "printing linens, calicoes, silks, &c., in figures, very lively and durable colors, and without the offensive smell which commonly attends linen-printing." Surely there was no lack of business ability on the distaff side of the Franklin house.

Boston women gave much assistance to their printer-husbands. Ezekiel Russel, the editor of that purely political publication, *The Censor*, was in addition a printer of chap-books and ballads which were sold from his stand near the Liberty Tree on Boston Common. His wife not only helped him in printing these, but she and another young woman of his household, having ready pens and a biddable muse, wrote with celerity popular and seasonable ballads on passing events, especially of tragic or funereal cast; and when these ballads were printed with a nice border of woodcuts of coffins and death's heads, they often had a long and profitable run of popularity. After his death, Widow

Russel still continued ballad making and monging.

It was given to a woman, Widow Margaret Draper, to publish the only newspaper which was issued in Boston during the siege, the *Massachusetts Gazette and Boston News Letter.* And a miserable little sheet it was, vari-colored, vari-typed, vari-sized; of such poor print that it is scarcely readable. When the British left Boston, Margaret Draper left also, and resided in England, where she received a pension from the British government.

The first newspaper in Pennsylvania was entitled *The American Weekly Mercury.* It was "imprinted by Andrew Bradford" in 1719. He was a son of the first newspaper printer in New York, William Bradford, Franklin's "cunning old fox," who lived to be ninety-two years old, and whose quaint tombstone may be seen in Trinity Churchyard. At Andrew's death in 1742, the paper appeared in mourning, and it was announced that it would be published by "the widow Bradford." She took in a partner, but speedily dropped him, and carried it on in her own name till 1746. During the time that Cor-

nelia Bradford printed this paper it was remarkable for its good type and neatness.

The Connecticut Courant and *The Centinel*
were both of them published for some years
by the widows of former proprietors.

The story of John Peter Zenger, the publisher of *The New York Weekly Journal*,
is one of the most interesting episodes in
our progress to free speech and liberty, but
cannot be dwelt on here. The feminine portion of his family was of assistance to him.
His daughter was mistress of a famous New
York tavern that saw many remarkable visitors, and heard much of the remarkable talk
of Zenger's friends. After his death in 1746,
his newspaper was carried on by his widow
for two years. Her imprint was, "New
York; Printed by the Widow Cathrine
Zenger at the Printing-Office in Stone
Street; Where Advertisements are taken
in, and all Persons may be supplied with this
Paper."

The whole number of newspapers printed
before the Revolution was not very large;
and when we see how readily and successfully this considerable number of women
assumed the cares of publishing, we know

that the "newspaper woman" of that day
was no rare or presumptuous creature, any
more than is the "newspaper-woman" of
our own day, albeit she was of very different
ilk ; but the spirit of independent self-reliance, when it became necessary to exhibit
self-reliance, was as prompt and as stable in
the feminine breast a century and a half ago
as now.   Then, as to-day, there were doubtless scores of good wives and daughters who
materially assisted their husbands in their
printing-shops, and whose work will never be
known.

There is no doubt that our great-grand-
mothers possessed wonderful ability to man-
age their own affairs, when it became necessary to do so, even in extended commercial
operations.   It is easy to trace in the New
England coast towns one influence which
tended to interest them, and make them capable of business transactions.   They constantly heard on all sides the discussion of
foreign trade, and were even encouraged to
enter into the discussion and the traffic.
They heard the Windward Islands, the Isle
of France, and Amsterdam, and Canton, and
the coast of Africa described by old travelled

mariners, by active young shipmasters, in a
way that put them far more in touch with
these far-away foreign shores, gave them
more knowledge of details of life in those
lands, than women of to-day have. And
women were encouraged, even urged, to take
an active share in foreign trade, in commercial speculation, by sending out a "venture"
whenever a vessel put out to sea, and whenever the small accumulation of money earned
by braiding straw, knitting stockings, selling
eggs or butter, or by spinning and weaving,
was large enough to be worth thus investing ;
and it needed not to be a very large sum to
be deemed proper for investment. When a
ship sailed out to China with cargo of gin-
seng, the ship's owner did not own all the
solid specie in the hold — the specie that was
to be invested in the rich and luxurious products of far Cathay. Complicated must have
been the accounts of these transactions, for
many were the parties in the speculation.
There were no giant monopolies in those
days. The kindly ship-owner permitted even
his humblest neighbor to share his profits.
And the profits often were large. The
stories of some of the voyages, the adven-

tures of the business contracts, read like a
fairy tale of commerce. In old letters may
be found reference to many of the ventures
sent by women. One young woman wrote
in 1759 : —

Inclos'd is a pair of Earrings Pleas ask
Captin Oliver to carry them a Ventur fer me if
he Thinks they will fetch anything to the Vally
of them ; tell him he may bring the effects in
anything he thinks will answer best.

One of the "effects" brought to this
young woman, and to hundreds of others,
was a certain acquaintance with business
transactions, a familiarity with the methods
of trade. When the father or husband died,
the woman could, if necessary, carry on his
business to a successful winding-up, or continue it in the future. Of the latter enterprise many illustrations might be given. In
the autumn of 1744 a large number of prominent business men in Newport went into a
storehouse on a wharf to examine the outfit
of a large privateer. A terrible explosion of
gunpowder took place, which killed nine of
them. One of the wounded was Sueton
Grant, a Scotchman, who had come to Amer-

ica in 1725. His wife, on hearing of the accident, ran at once to the dock, took in at a
glance the shocking scene and its demands
for assistance, and cutting into strips her
linen apron with the housewife's scissors she
wore at her side, calmly bound up the wounds
of her dying husband. Mr. Grant was at this
time engaged in active business ; he had
agencies in Europe, and many privateers
afloat. Mrs. Grant took upon her shoulders
these great responsibilities, and successfully
carried them on for many years, while she educated her children, and cared for her home.

A good example of her force of character
was once shown in a court of law. She had
an important litigation on hand and large
interests at stake, when she discovered the
duplicity of her counsel, and her consequent
danger. She went at once to the court-
room where the case was being tried ; when
her lawyer promptly but vainly urged her to
retire. The judge, disturbed by the inter-
ruption, asked for an explanation, and Mrs.
Grant at once unfolded the knavery of her
counsel and asked permission to argue her
own case. Her dignity, force, and lucidity
so moved the judge that he permitted her to

address the jury, which she did in so convincing a manner as to cause them to promptly render a verdict favorable to her. She passed through some trying scenes at the time of the Revolution with wonderful decision and ability, and received from every one the respect and deference due to a thorough business man, though she was a woman.

In New York the feminine Dutch blood showed equal capacity in business matters; and it is said that the management of considerable estates and affairs often was assumed by widows in New Amsterdam. Two noted examples are Widow De Vries and Widow Provoost. The former was married in 1659, to Rudolphus De Vries, and after his death she carried on his Dutch trade — not only buying and selling foreign goods, but going repeatedly to Holland in the position of supercargo on her own ships. She married Frederick Phillipse, and it was through her keenness and thrift and her profitable business, as well as through his own success, that Phillipse became the richest man in the colony and acquired the largest West Indian trade.

Widow Maria Provoost was equally successful at the beginning of the eighteenth
century, and had a vast Dutch business correspondence. Scarce a ship from Spain,
the Mediterranean, or the West Indies, but
brought her large consignments of goods.
She too married a second time, and as
Madam James Alexander filled a most dignified position in New York, being the only
person besides the Governor to own a two-
horse coach. Her house was the finest in
town, and such descriptions of its various
apartments as " the great drawing-room, the
lesser drawing - room, the blue and gold
leather room, the green and gold leather
room, the chintz room, the great tapestry
room, the little front parlour, the back parlour," show its size and pretensions.

Madam Martha Smith, widow of Colonel
William Smith of St. George's Manor, Long
Island, was a woman of affairs in another
field. In an interesting memorandum left
by her we read : —

Jan ye 16, 1707. My company killed a yearling whale made 27 barrels. Feb ye 4, Indian
Harry with his boat struck a whale and called
for my boat to help him. I had but a third which

was 4 barrels. Feb 22, my two boats & my sons
and Floyds boats killed a yearling whale of which
I had half — made 36 barrels, my share 18 barrels. Feb 24 my company killed a school whale
which made 35 barrels. March 13, my company
killed a small yearling made 30 barrels. March
17, my company killed two yearlings in one day ;
one made 27, the other 14 barrels.

We find her paying to Lord Cornbury fifteen pounds, a duty on "ye 20th part of her
eyle." And she apparently succeeded in her
enterprises.

In early Philadelphia directories may be
found the name of "Margaret Duncan,
Merchant, No. 1 S. Water St." This capable woman had been shipwrecked on her
way to the new world. In the direst hour
of that extremity, when forced to draw lots
for the scant supply of food, she vowed to
build a church in her new home if her life
should be spared. The "Vow Church" in
Philadelphia, on Thirteenth Street near Market Street, for many years proved her fulfilment of this vow, and also bore tribute to
the prosperity of this pious Scotch Presbyterian in her adopted home.

Southern women were not outstripped by

the business women of the north. No more practical woman ever lived in America than Eliza Lucas Pinckney. When a young girl she resided on a plantation at Wappoo, South Carolina, owned by her father, George Lucas. He was Governor of Antigua, and observing her fondness for and knowledge of botany, and her intelligent power of application of her knowledge, he sent to her many tropical seeds and plants for her amusement and experiment in her garden. Among the seeds were some of indigo, which she became convinced could be profitably grown in South Carolina. She at once determined to experiment, and planted indigo seed in March, 1741. The young plants started finely, but were cut down by an unusual frost. She planted seed a second time, in April, and these young indigo-plants were destroyed by worms. Notwithstanding these discouragements, she tried a third time, and with success. Her father was delighted with her enterprise and persistence, and when he learned that the indigo had seeded and ripened, sent an Englishman named Cromwell — an experienced indigo-worker — from Montserrat to teach his

daughter Eliza the whole process of extracting the dye from the weed. Vats were built
on Wappoo Creek, in which was made the
first indigo formed in Carolina. It was of
indifferent quality, for Cromwell feared the
successful establishment of the industry in
America would injure the indigo trade in
his own colony, so he made a mystery of the
process, and put too much lime in the vats,
doubtless thinking he could impose upon a
woman. But Miss Lucas watched him carefully, and in spite of his duplicity, and
doubtless with considerable womanly power
of guessing, finally obtained a successful
knowledge and application of the complex
and annoying methods of extracting indigo,
— methods which required the untiring attention of sleepless nights, and more "judgment" than intricate culinary triumphs.
After the indigo was thoroughly formed by
steeping, beating, and washing, and taken
from the vats, the trials of the maker were
not over. It must be exposed to the sun, but
if exposed too much it would be burnt, if
too little it would rot. Myriads of flies col-
lected around it and if unmolested would
quickly ruin it. If packed too soon it would

sweat and disintegrate. So, from the first moment the tender plant appeared above ground, when the vast clouds of destroying grasshoppers had to be annihilated by flocks of hungry chickens, or carefully dislodged by watchful human care, indigo culture and manufacture was a distressing worry, and was made still more unalluring to a feminine experimenter by the fact that during the weary weeks it laid in the "steepers" and "beaters" it gave forth a most villainously offensive smell.

Soon after Eliza Lucas' hard-earned success she married Charles Pinckney, and it is pleasant to know that her father gave her, as part of her wedding gift, all the indigo on the plantation. She saved the whole crop for seed, — and it takes about a bushel of indigo seed to plant four acres, — and she planted the Pinckney plantation at Ashepoo, and gave to her friends and neighbors small quantities of seed for individual experiment ; all of which proved successful. The culture of indigo at once became universal, the newspapers were full of instructions upon the subject, and the dye was exported to England by 1747, in such quantity that merchants trading in Carolina petitioned Parliament for a bounty on Carolina indigo. An act of Parliament was passed allowing a bounty of sixpence a pound on indigo raised in the British-American plantations and imported directly to Great Britain. Spurred on by this wise act, the planters applied with re-doubled vigor to the production of the article, and soon received vast profits as the rewards of their labor and care. It is said that just previous to the Revolution more children were sent from South Carolina to England to receive educations, than from all the other colonies, — and this through the profits of indigo and rice. Many indigo planters doubled their capital every three or four years, and at last not only England was sup-plied with indigo from South Carolina, but the Americans undersold the French in many European markets. It exceeded all other southern industries in importance, and became a general medium of exchange. When General Marion's young nephew was sent to school at Philadelphia, he started off with a wagon-load of indigo to pay his ex-penses. The annual dues of the Winyah Indigo Society of Georgetown were paid in the dye, and the society had grown so wealthy in 1753, that it established a large charity school and valuable library.

Ramsay, the historian of South Carolina, wrote in 1808, that the indigo trade proved more beneficial to Carolina than the mines of Mexico or Peru to old or new Spain. By the year of his writing, however, indigo (without waiting for extermination through its modern though less reliable rivals, the aniline dyes) had been driven out of Southern plantations by its more useful and profitable field neighbor, King Cotton, that had been set on a throne by the invention of a Yankee schoolmaster. The time of greatest production and export of indigo was just previous to the Revolution, and at one time it was worth four or five dollars a pound. And to-day only the scanty records of the indigo trade, a few rotting cypress boards of the steeping-vats, and the blue-green leaves of the wild wayside indigo, remain of all this prosperity to show the great industry founded by this remarkable and intelligent woman.

The rearing of indigo was not this young girl's only industry. I will quote from various letters written by her in 1741 and 1742 before her marriage, to show her many duties, her intelligence, her versatility : —

Wrote my father on the pains I had taken to bring the Indigo, Ginger, Cotton, Lucern, and Casada to perfection and had greater hopes from the Indigo, if I could have the seed earlier, than any of ye rest of ye things I had tried.

I have the burthen of 3 Plantations to transact which requires much writing and more business and fatigue of other sorts than you can imagine. But lest you should imagine it too burthensome to a girl in my early time of life, give me leave to assure you I think myself happy that I can be useful to so good a father.

Wont you laugh at me if I tell you I am so busy in providing for Posterity I hardly allow myself time to eat or sleep, and can but just snatch a moment to write to you and a friend or two more. I am making a large plantation of oaks which I look upon as my own property whether my father gives me the land or not, and therefore I design many yeer hence when oaks are more valuable than they are now, which you know they will be when we come to build fleets. I intend I say two thirds of the produce of my oaks for a charity (Ill tell you my scheme another time) and the other third for those that shall have the trouble to put my design in execution.

I have a sister to instruct, and a parcel of little negroes whom I have undertaken to teach to read.

The Cotton, Guinea Corn, and Ginger planted was cutt off by a frost. I wrote you in a former letter we had a good crop of Indigo upon the ground. I make no doubt this will prove a valuable commodity in time. Sent Gov. Thomas daughter a tea chest of my own doing.

I am engaged with the Rudiments of Law to which I am but a stranger. If you will not laugh too immoderately at me I'll trust you with a Secrett. I have made two Wills already. I know I have done no harm for I conn'd my Lesson perfect. A widow hereabouts with a pretty little fortune teazed me intolerably to draw a marriage settlement, but it was out of my depth and I absolutely refused it — so she got an able hand to do it — indeed she could afford it — but I could not get off being one of the Trustees to her settlement, and an old Gent^n the other. I shall begin to think myself an old woman before I am a young one, having such mighty affairs on my hands.

I think this record of important work could scarce be equalled by any young girl in a comparative station of life nowadays. And when we consider the trying circumstances, the difficult conditions, in which these varied enterprises were carried on, we can well be amazed at the story.

Indigo was not the only important staple which attracted Mrs. Pinckney's attention, and the manufacture of which she made a success. In 1755 she carried with her to England enough rich silk fabric, which she had raised and spun and woven herself in the vicinity of Charleston, to make three fine silk gowns, one of which was presented to the Princess Dowager of Wales, and another to Lord Chesterfield. This silk was said to be equal in beauty to any silk ever imported.

This was not the first American silk that had graced the person of English royalty. In 1734 the first windings of Georgia silk had been taken from the filature to England, and the queen wore a dress made thereof at the king's next birthday. Still earlier in the field Virginia had sent its silken tribute to royalty. In the college library at Williams-burg, Va., may be seen a letter signed " Charles R." — his most Gracious Majesty Charles the Second. It was written by his

Majesty's private secretary, and addressed to Governor Berkeley for the king's loyal subjects in Virginia. It reads thus:—

Trusty and Well beloved, We Greet you Well. Wee have received wth much content ye dutifull respects of Our Colony in ye present lately made us by you & ye councill there, of ye first product of ye new Manufacture of Silke, which as a marke of Our Princely acceptation of yor duteys & for yor particular encouragement, etc. Wee have been commanded to be wrought up for ye use of Our Owne Person.

And earliest of all is the tradition, dear to the hearts of Virginians, that Charles I. was crowned in 1625 in a robe woven of Virginia silk. The Queen of George III. was the last English royalty to be similarly honored, for the next attack of the silk fever produced a suit for an American ruler, George Washington.

The culture of silk in America was an industry calculated to attract the attention of women, and indeed was suited to them, but men were not exempt from the fever; and the history of the manifold and undaunted efforts of governor's councils, parliaments, noblemen, philosophers, and kings to force silk culture in America forms one of the most curious examples extant of persistent and futile efforts to run counter to positive economic conditions, for certainly physical conditions are fairly favorable.

South Carolina women devoted themselves with much success to agricultural experiments. Henry Laurens brought from Italy and naturalized the olive-tree, and his daughter, Martha Laurens Ramsay, experimented with the preservation of the fruit until her productions equalled the imported olives. Catharine Laurens Ramsay manufactured opium of the first quality. In 1755 Henry Laurens' garden in Ansonborough was enriched with every curious vegetable product from remote quarters of the world that his extensive mercantile connections enabled him to procure, and the soil and climate of South Carolina to cherish. He introduced besides olives, capers, limes, ginger, guinea grass, Alpine strawberries (bearing nine months in the year), and many choice varieties of fruits. This garden was superintended by his wife, Mrs. Elinor Laurens.

Mrs. Martha Logan was a famous botanist and florist. She was born in 1702, and was the daughter of Robert Daniel, one of the last proprietary governors of South Carolina. When fourteen years old, she married George Logan, and all her life treasured a beautiful and remarkable garden. When seventy years old, she compiled from her knowledge and experience a regular treatise on gardening, which was published after her death, with the title *The Garden's Kalendar.* It was for many years the standard work on gardening in that locality.

Mrs. Hopton and Mrs. Lamboll were early and assiduous flower-raisers and experimenters in the eighteenth century, and Miss Maria Drayton, of Drayton Hall, a skilled botanist.

The most distinguished female botanist of colonial days was Jane Colden, the daughter of Governor Cadwallader Colden, of New York. Her love of the science was inherited from her father, the friend and correspondent of Linnæus, Collinson, and other botanists. She learned a method of taking leaf-impressions in printers' ink, and sent careful impressions of American plants and leaves to the European collectors. John Ellis wrote of her to Linnæus in April, 1758 : —

This young lady merits your esteem, and does honor to your system. She has drawn and described four hundred plants in your method. Her father has a plant called after her Coldenia. Suppose you should call this new genus Coldenella or any other name which might distinguish her.

Peter Collinson said also that she was the first lady to study the Linnæan system, and deserved to be celebrated. Another tribute to her may be found in a letter of Walter Rutherford's : —

From the middle of the Woods this Family corresponds with all the learned Societies in Europe. His daughter Jenny is a Florist and Botanist. She has discovered a great number of Plants never before described and has given their Properties and Virtues, many of which are found useful in Medicine and she draws and colours them with great Beauty. Dr. Whyte of Edinburgh is in the number of her correspondents.

N. B. She makes the best cheese I ever ate in America.

The homely virtue of being a good cheese-
maker was truly a saving clause to
palliate and excuse so much
feminine scientific
knowledge.

CHAPTER III.

"DOUBLE-TONGUED AND NAUGHTY WOMEN."

I AM much impressed in reading the court records of those early days, to note the vast care taken in all the colonies to prevent lying, slandering, gossiping, backbiting, and idle babbling, or, as they termed it, "brabling;" to punish "common sowers and movers"— of dissensions, I suppose.

The loving neighborliness which proved as strong and as indispensable a foundation for a successful colony as did godliness, made the settlers resent deeply any violations, though petty, of the laws of social kindness. They felt that what they termed "opprobrious schandalls tending to defamaçon and disparagment" could not be endured.

One old author declares that "blabbing, babbling, tale-telling, and discovering the faults and frailities of others is a most Common and evill practice." He asserts that a woman should be a "main store house of secresie, a Maggazine of taciturnitie, the closet of connivence, the mumbudget of silence, the cloake bagge of rouncell, the capcase, fardel, or pack of friendly toleration;" which, as a whole, seems to be a good deal to ask. Men were, as appears by the records, more frequently brought up for these offences of the tongue, but women were not spared either in indictment or punishment. In Windsor, Conn., one woman was whipped for " wounding" a neighbor, not in the flesh, but in the sensibilities.

In 1652 Joane Barnes, of Plymouth, Mass., was indicted for "slandering," and sentenced "to sitt in the stockes during the Courts pleasure, and a paper whereon her facte written in Capitall letters to be made faste vnto her hatt or neare vnto her all the tyme of her sitting there." In 1654 another Joane in Northampton County, Va., suffered a peculiarly degrading punishment for slander. She was " drawen ouer the Kings Creeke at the starne of a boate or Canoux, also the next Saboth day in the tyme of diuine seruis" was obliged to present herself before the minister and congregation, and acknow-

ledge her fault, and ask forgiveness. This
was an old Scotch custom. The same year
one Charlton called the parson, Mr. Cotton,
a "black cotted rascal," and was punished
therefor in the same way. Richard Buckland,
for writing a slanderous song about Ann
Smith, was similarly pilloried, bearing a paper
on his hat inscribed *Inimicus Libellus*, and
since possibly all the church attendants did
not know Latin, to publicly beg Ann's forgiveness in English for his libellous poesy.
The punishment of offenders by exposing
them, wrapped in sheets, or attired in foul
clothing, on the stool of repentance in the
meeting-house in time of divine service, has
always seemed to me specially bitter, unseemly, and unbearable.

It should be noted that these suits for
slander were between persons in every station of life. When Anneke Jans Bogardus
(wife of Dominie Bogardus, the second established clergyman in New Netherlands), would
not remain in the house with one Grietje van
Salee, a woman of doubtful reputation, the
latter told throughout the neighborhood that
Anneke had lifted her petticoats when cross-
ing the street, and exposed her ankles in un-

seemly fashion; and she also said that the
Dominie had sworn a false oath. Action for
slander was promptly begun, and witnesses
produced to show that Anneke had flourished
her petticoats no more than was seemly
and tidy to escape the mud. Judgment was
pronounced against Grietje and her husband. She had to make public declaration
in the Fort that she had lied, and to pay
three guilders. The husband had to pay
a fine, and swear to the good character of
the Dominie and good carriage of the Dominie's wife, and he was not permitted to
carry weapons in town, — a galling punishment.

Dominie Bogardus was in turn sued several times for slander, — once by Thomas
Hall, the tobacco planter, simply for saying
that Thomas' tobacco was bad; and again,
wonderful to relate, by one of his deacons —
Deacon Van Cortlandt.

Special punishment was provided for
women. Old Dr. Johnson said gruffly to a
lady friend: "Madam, there are different
ways of restraining evil; stocks for men, a
ducking-stool for women, pounds for beasts."
The old English instrument of punishment,

— as old as the Doomsday survey, — the cucking-stool or ducking-stool, was in vogue here, was insultingly termed a "publique convenience," and was used in the Southern and Central colonies for the correction of common scolds. We read in Blackstone's *Commentaries*, "A common scold may be indicted and if convicted shall be sentenced to be placed in a certain engine of correction called the trebucket, castigatory, or cucking-stool." Still another name for this "engine" was a "gum-stool." The brank, or scold's bridle, — a cruel and degrading means of punishment employed in England for "curst queans" as lately as 1824, — was unknown in America. A brank may be seen at the Guildhall in Worcester, England. One at Walton-on-Thames bears the date 1633. On the Isle of Man, when the brank was removed, the wearer had to say thrice, in public, "Tongue, thou hast lied." I do not find that women ever had to "run the gaunt-elope" as did male offenders in 1685 in Boston, and, though under another name, in several of the provinces.

Women in Maine were punished by being gagged; in Plymouth, Mass., and in Easthampton, L. I., they had cleft sticks placed on their tongues in public; in the latter place because the dame said her husband "had brought her to a place where there was neither gospel nor magistracy." In Salem "one Oliver — his wife" had a cleft stick placed on her tongue for half an hour in public "for reproaching the elders." It was a high offence to speak "discornfully" of the elders and magistrates.

The first volume of the *American Historical Record* gives a letter said to have been written to Governor Endicott, of Massachusetts, in 1634 by one Thomas Hartley from Hungar's Parish, Virginia. It gives a graphic description of a ducking-stool, and an account of a ducking in Virginia. I quote from it : —

The day afore yesterday at two of ye clock in ye afternoon I saw this punishment given to one Betsey wife of John Tucker, who by ye violence of her tongue had made his house and ye neighborhood uncomfortable. She was taken to ye pond where I am sojourning by ye officer who was joyned by ye magistrate and ye Minister Mr. Cotton, who had frequently admonished her and a large number of People. They had a machine for ye purpose y^t belongs to ye Parish, and which I was so told had been so used three times this Summer.   It is a platform with 4 small rollers or wheels and two upright posts between which works a Lever by a Rope fastened to its shorter or heavier end.   At the end of ye longer arm is fixed a stool upon which s^d Betsey was fastened by cords, her gown tied fast around her feete. The Machine was then moved up to ye edge of ye pond, ye Rope was slackened by ye officer and ye woman was allowed to go down under ye water for ye space of half a minute.   Betsey had a stout stomach, and would not yield until she had allowed herself to be ducked 5 severall times. At length she cried piteously Let me go Let me go, by Gods help I 'll sin no more.   Then they drew back ye machine, untied ye Ropes and let her walk home in her wetted clothes a hopefully penitent woman.

I have seen an old chap-book print of a ducking-stool with a "light huswife of the banck-side" in it.   It was rigged much like an old-fashioned well-sweep, the woman and chair occupying the relative place of the bucket.   The base of the upright support was on a low-wheeled platform.

Bishop Meade, in his *Old Churches, Ministers, and Families of Virginia*, tells of one

"scolding quean" who was ordered to be
ducked three times from a vessel lying in
James River. Places for ducking were prepared near the Court Houses. The marshal's
fee for ducking was only two pounds of tobacco. The ducking-stools were not kept in
church porches, as in England. In 1634 two
women were sentenced to be either drawn
from King's Creek "from one Cowpen to another at the starn of a boat or kanew," or to
present themselves before the congregation,
and ask forgiveness of each other and God.
In 1633 it was ordered that a ducking-stool
be built in every county in Maryland. At a
court-baron at St. Clements, the county was
prosecuted for not having one of these "public conveniences." In February, 1775, a
ducking-stool was ordered to be placed at the
confluence of the Ohio and Monongahela
Rivers, and was doubtless used. As late as
1819 Georgia women were ducked in the
Oconee River for scolding. And in 1824, at
the court of Quarter Sessions, a Philadelphia
woman was sentenced to be ducked, but the
punishment was not inflicted, as it was
deemed obsolete and contrary to the spirit
of the times. In 1803 the ducking-stool was

still used in Liverpool, England, and in 1809 in Leominster, England.

One of the last indictments for ducking in our own country was that of Mrs. Anne Royall in Washington, almost in our own day. She was a hated lobbyist, whom Mr. Forney called an itinerant virago, and who became so abusive to congressmen that she was indicted as a common scold before Judge William Cranch, and was sentenced by him to be ducked in the Potomac. She was, however, released with a fine.

Women curst with a shrewish tongue were often punished in Puritan colonies. In 1647 it was ordered that "common scoulds" be punished in Rhode Island by ducking, but I find no records of the punishment being given. In 1649 several women were prosecuted in Salem, Mass., for scolding ; and on May 15, 1672, the General Court of Massachusetts ordered that scolds and railers should be gagged or "set in a ducking-stool and dipped over head and ears three times," but I do not believe that this law was ever executed in Massachusetts. Nor was it in Maine, though in 1664 a dozen towns were fined forty shillings each for having no "coucking-stool." Equally severe punishments were inflicted for other crimes. Katharine Ainis, of Plymouth, was publicly whipped on training day, and ordered to wear a large B cut in red cloth "sewed to her vper garment." In 1637 Dorothy Talbye, a Salem dame, for beating her husband was ordered to be bound and chained to a post. At a later date she was whipped, and then was hanged for killing her child, who bore the strange name of Difficulty. No one but a Puritan magistrate could doubt, from Winthrop's account of her, that she was insane. Another "audatious" Plymouth shrew, for various "vncivill carriages" to her husband, was sentenced to the pillory; and if half that was told of her was true, she richly deserved her sentence; but, as she displayed "greate pensiveness and sorrow" before the simple Pilgrim magistrates, she escaped temporarily, to be punished at a later date for a greater sin. The magistrates firmly asserted in court and out that "meekness is ye chojsest orniment for a woman."

Joane Andrews sold in York, Maine, in 1676, two stones in a firkin of butter. For this cheatery she "stood in towne meeting at York and at towne meeting at Kittery till 2 hours bee expended, with her offense written upon a paper in capitall letters on her forehead." The court record of one woman delinquent in Plymouth, in 1683, is grimly comic. It seems that Mary Rosse exercised what was called by the "painful" court chronicler in a triumph of orthographical and nomenclatory art, an " inthewsiastickall power " over one Shingleterry, a married man, who cringingly pleaded, as did our first father Adam, that "hee must doo what shee bade him " — or, in modern phrase, that she hypnotized him. Mary Rosse and her uncanny power did not receive the consideration that similar witches and works do nowadays. She was publicly whipped and sent home to her mother, while her hypnotic subject was also whipped, and I presume sent home to his wife.

It should be noted that in Virginia, under the laws proclaimed by Argall, women were in some ways tenderly regarded. They were not punished for absenting themselves from church on Sundays or holidays; while men for one offence of this nature had "to lie neck and heels that night, and be a slave to the colony for the following week; for the second offence to be a slave for a month; for the third, for a year and a day."

It is curious to see how long and how constantly, in spite of their severe and manifold laws, the pious settlers could suffer through certain ill company which they had been unlucky enough to bring over, provided the said offenders did not violate the religious rules of the community. We might note as ignoble instances, Will Fancie and his wife, of New Haven, and John Dandy and his wife, of Maryland. Their names constantly appear for years in the court records, as offenders and as the cause of offences. John Dandy at one time swore in court that all his "controversies from the beginning of the World to this day" had ceased; but it would have been more to the purpose had he also added till the end of the world, for his violence soon brought him to the gallows. Will Fancie's wife seemed capable of any and every offence, from "stealing pinnes" to stealing the affections of nearly every man with whom she chanced to be thrown; and the magistrates of New Haven were evidently sorely puzzled how to deal with her.

I have noted in the court or church records of all witch-ridden communities, save in the records of poor crazed and bewildered Salem, where the flame was blown into a roaring blaze by "the foolish breath of Cotton Mather," that there always appear on the pages some plain hints, and usually some definite statements, which account for the accusation of witchcraft against individuals. And these hints indicate a hated personality of the witch. To illustrate my meaning, let me take the the case of Goody Garlick, of Easthampton, Long Island. In reading the early court records of that town, I was impressed with the constant meddlesome interference of this woman in all social and town matters. Every page reeked of Garlick. She was an ever-ready witness in trespass, boundary, and slander suits, for she was apparently on hand everywhere. She was present when a young man made ugly faces at the wife of Lion Gardiner, because she scolded him for eating up her "pomkin porage;" and she was listening when Mistress Edwards was called a base liar, because she asserted she had in her chest a new petticoat that she had brought from England some years before, and had never worn (and of course no woman could believe that). In short, Goody Garlick was a constant tale-bearer and barrator. Hence it was not surprising to me to find, when Mistress Arthur Howell, Lion Gardiner's daughter, fell suddenly and strangely ill, and cried out that "a double-tongued naughty woman was tormenting her, a woman who had a black cat," that the wise neighbors at once remembered that Goody Garlick was double-tongued and naughty, and had a black cat. She was speedily indicted for witchcraft, and the gravamen appeared to be her constant tale-bearing.

In 1706 a Virginian goody with a prettier name, Grace Sherwood, was tried as a witch; and with all the superstition of the day, and the added superstition of the surrounding and rapidly increasing negro population, there were but three Virginian witch-trials. Grace Sherwood's name was also of constant recurrence in court annals, from the year 1690, on the court records of Princess Anne County, especially in slander cases. She was examined, after her indictment, for "witches marks" by a jury of twelve matrons, each of whom testified that Grace was "not like yur." The magistrates seem to have been somewhat disconcerted at the convicting testimony of this jury, and at a loss how to proceed, but the witch asserted her willingness to endure trial by water. A day was set for the ducking, but it rained, and the tenderly considerate court thought the weather unfavorable for the trial on account of the danger to Grace's health, and postponed the ducking. At last, on a sunny July day, when she could not take cold, the witch was securely pinioned and thrown into Lyn Haven Bay, with directions from the magistrates to "but her into the debth." Into the "debth" of the water she should have contentedly and innocently sunk, but "contrary to the Judgments of all the spectators" she persisted in swimming, and at last was fished out and again examined to see whether the "witches marks" were washed off. One of the examiners was certainly far from being prepossessed in Grace's favor. She was a dame who eight years before had testified that "Grace came to her one night, and rid her, and went out of the key hole or crack in the door like a black cat." Grace Sherwood was not executed, and she did not die of the ducking, but it cooled her quarrelsome temper. She lived till 1740. The point where she was butted into the depth is to this day called Witches Duck.

Grace Sherwood was not the only poor soul that passed through the "water-test" or "the fleeting on the water" for witchcraft. In September, 1692, in Fairfield, Conn., the accused witches "Mercy Disburrow and Elizabeth Clauson were bound hand and foot and put into the water, and they swam like cork, and one labored to press them into the water, and they buoyed up like cork." Many cruel scenes were enacted in Connecticut, none more so than the persistent inquisition of Goodwife Knapp after she was condemned to death for witchcraft. She was constantly tormented by her old friends and neighbors to confess and to accuse one Goody Staples as an accomplice; but the poor woman repeated that she must not wrong any one nor say anything untrue. She added : —

The truth is you would have me say that goodwife Staples is a witch but I have sins enough to answer for already, I know nothing against goodwife Staples and I hope she is an honest woman.

You know not what I know. I have been fished withall in private more than you are aware of. I apprehend that goodwife Staples hath done me wrong in her testimony but I must not return evil for evil.

Being still urged and threatened with eternal damnation, she finally burst into bitter tears, and begged her persecutors to cease, saying in words that must have lingered long in their memory, and that still make the heart ache, " Never, never was poor creature tempted as I am tempted ! oh pray ! pray for me ! "

The last scene in this New England tragedy was when her poor dead body was cut down from the gallows, and laid upon the green turf beside her grave ; and her old neighbors, excited with superstition, and blinded to all sense of shame or unwomanliness, crowded about examining eagerly for " witch signs ; " while in the foreground Goodwife Staples, whose lying words had hanged her friend, kneeled by the poor insulted corpse, weeping and wringing her hands, calling upon God, and asserting the innocence of the murdered woman.

It is a curious fact that, in an era which

did not much encourage the public speech or public appearance of women, they should have served on juries; yet they occasionally did, not only in witchcraft cases such as Grace Sherwood's and Alice Cartwright's, — another Virginia witch, — but in murder cases, as in Kent County, Maryland; these juries were not usually to render the final decision, but to decide upon certain points, generally purely personal, by which their wise husbands could afterwards be guided. I don't know that these female juries shine as exemplars of wisdom and judgment. In 1693 a jury of twelve women in Newbury, Mass., rendered this decision, which certainly must have been final : —

Wee judge according to our best lights and contients that the Death of said Elizabeth was not by any violens or wrong done to her by any parson or thing but by some soden stoping of hir Breath.

In Revolutionary days a jury of "twelve discreet matrons" of Worcester, Mass., gave a decision in the case of Bathsheba Spooner, which was found after her execution to be a wrong judgment. She was the last woman hanged by law in Massachusetts, and her

cruel fate may have proved a vicarious suffering and means of exemption for other
women criminals.

Women, as well as men, when suspected
murderers, had to go through the cruel and
shocking "blood-ordeal." This belief, supported by the assertions of that learned fool,
King James, in his *Demonologie*, lingered
long in the minds of many, — indeed does
to this day in poor superstitious folk. The
royal author says : —

In a secret murther, if the dead carkas be at
any time thereafter handled by the murtherer, it
will gush out of blood.

Sometimes a great number of persons were
made to touch in turn the dead body, hoping
thus to discover the murderer.

It has been said that few women were
taught to write in colonial days, and that
those few wrote so ill their letters could
scarce be read. I have seen a goodly number of letters written by women in those
times, and the handwriting is comparatively
as good as that of their husbands and brothers. Margaret Winthrop wrote with pre-
cision and elegance. A letter of Anne

Winthrop's dated 1737 is clear, regular, and beautiful. Mary Higginson's writing is fair, and Elizabeth Cushing's irregular and uncertain, as if of infrequent occurrence. Elizabeth Corwin's is clear, though irregular; Mehitable Parkman's more careless and wavering; all are easily read. But the most beautiful old writing I have ever seen, — elegant, regular, wonderfully clear and well-proportioned, was written by the hand of a woman, — a criminal, a condemned murderer, Elizabeth Attwood, who was executed in 1720 for the murder of her infant child. The letter was written from "Ipswitch Gole in Bonds" to Cotton Mather, and is a most pathetic and intelligent appeal for his interference to save her life. The beauty and simplicity of her language, the force and directness of her expressions, her firm denial of the crime, her calm religious assurance, are most touching to read, even after the lapse of centuries, and make one wonder that any one — magistrate or priest, — even Cotton Mather — could doubt her innocence. But she was hanged before a vast concourse of eager people, and was declared most impenitent and bold in her denial of her guilt;

and it was brought up against her, as a most hardened brazenry, that to cheat the hangman (who always took as handsel of his victim the garments in which she was "turned off"), she appeared in her worst attire, and announced that he would get but a sorry suit from her. I do not know the estate in life of Elizabeth Attwood, but it could not have been mean, for her letter shows great refinement.

CHAPTER IV.

ACCOUNTS of isolated figures are often more interesting than chapters of general history, and biographies more attractive than state records, because more petty details of vivid human interest can be learned; so, in order to present clearly a picture of the social life of women in the earliest days of New England, I give a description of a group of women, contiguous in residence, and contemporary in life, rather than an account of some special dame of dignity or note; and I call this group Boston Neighbors.

If the setting of this picture would add to its interest, it is easy to portray the little settlement. The peninsula, but half as large as the Boston of to-day, was fringed with sea-marshes, and was crowned with three conical hills, surmounted respectively with the wind-mill, the fort, and the beacon. The champaign was simply an extended pasture with

few trees, but fine springs of water. Wind-
ing footpaths — most interesting of roadways
— connected the detached dwellings, and
their irregular outlines still show in our Boston streets. The thatched clay houses were
being replaced by better and more substantial dwellings. William Coddington had built
the first brick house.

On the main street, now Washington
Street, just east of where the Old South
Church now stands, lived the dame of highest degree, and perhaps the most beautiful
personality, in this little group — Margaret
Tyndal Winthrop, the " loving faythfull yoke-
fellow" of Governor John Winthrop. She
was his third wife, though he was but thirty
when he married her. He had been first
married when but seventeen years old. He
writes that he was conceived by his parents
to be at that age a man in stature and understanding. This wife brought to him, and left
to him, " a large portion of outward estate,"
and four little children. Of the second wife
he writes, " For her carriage towards myselfe,
it was so amiable and observant as I am not
able to expresse ; it had only this inconven-
ience, that it made me delight in hir too much

to enjoy hir long," — and she lived with him but a year and a day. He married Margaret in 1618, and when she had borne five children, he left her in 1630, and sailed to New England. She came also the following year, and was received "with great joy" and a day of Thanksgiving. For the remaining sixteen years of her life she had but brief separations from her husband, and she died, as he wrote, "especially beloved of all the country." Her gentle love-letters to her husband, and the simple testimony of contemporary letters of her relatives and friends, show her to have been truly "a sweet gracious woman" who endured the hardships of her new home, the Governor's loss of fortune, and his trying political experiences, with unvarying patience and "singular virtue, modesty and piety."

There lived at this time in Boston a woman who must have been well known personally by Madam Winthrop, for she was a near neighbor, living within stone's throw of the Governor's house, on the spot where now stands "The Old Corner Bookstore." This woman was Anne Hutchinson. She came with Rev. John Cotton from Boston, England, to Boston, New England, well respected and well beloved. She went an outcast, hated and feared by many she left behind her in Boston. For years her name was on every tongue, while she was under repeated trials and examinations for heresy. In the controversy over her and her doctrines, magistrates, ministers, women, soldiers, the common multitude of Boston, all took part, and took sides; through the pursuance of the controversy the government of the colony was changed. Her special offences against doctrines were those two antiquated "heresies," Antinomianism and Familism, which I could hardly define if I would. According to Winthrop they were "those two dangerous errors that the person of the Holy Ghost dwells in a justified person, and that no sanctification can help to evidence to us our justification." Her special offences against social and religious routines were thus related by Cotton Mather : —

At the meetings of the women which used to be called gossippings it was her manner to carry on very pious discourses and so put the neighborhood upon examining their spiritual estates by telling them how far a person might go in "trou-

ble of mind," and being restrained from very
many evils and constrained into very many duties,
by none but a legal work upon their souls without ever coming to a saving union with the Lord
Jesus Christ, that many of them were convinced
of a very great defect in the settlement of their
everlasting peace, and acquainted more with the
"Spirit of the Gospel" than ever they were
before.   This mighty show and noise of devotion
made the reputation of a non-such among the
people until at length under pretence of that
warrant "that the elder women are to teach the
younger" she set up weekly meetings at her
house whereto three score or four score people
would report. . . .

It was not long before it was found out that
most of the errors then crawling like vipers were
hatch'd at these meetings.

So disturbed was the synod of ministers
which was held early in the controversy, that
this question was at once resolved : —

That though women might meet (some few together) to pray and edify one another, yet such a
set assembly (as was then the practice in Boston)
where sixty or more did meet every week, and
one woman (in a prophetical way by resolving
questions of doctrines and expounding scripture)

took upon her the whole exercise, was agreed to
be disorderly and without rule.

As I read the meagre evidences of her
belief, I see that Anne Hutchinson had a
high supernatural faith which, though mysti-
cal at its roots, aimed at being practical in
its fruits ; but she was critical, tactless, and
over-inquisitive, and doubtless censorious,
and worst of all she "vented her revelations," which made her seem to many of the
Puritans the very essence of fanaticism ; so
she was promptly placed on trial for heresy
for "twenty-nine cursed opinions and falling
into fearful lying, with an impudent Forehead
in the public assembly." The end of it all
in that theocracy could not be uncertain.
One woman, even though her followers included Governor Sir Henry Vane, and a
hundred of the most influential men of the
community, could not stop the powerful ma-
chinery of the Puritan Church and Commonwealth, the calm, well-planned opposition of
Winthrop ; and after a succession of mortifying indignities, and unlimited petty hectoring
and annoying, she was banished. "The court
put an end to her vapouring talk, and finding
no hope of reclaiming her from her scandal-

ous, dangerous, and enchanting extravagancies, ordered her out of the colony."

In reading of her life, her trials, it is difficult to judge whether — to borrow Howel's expression — the crosier or the distaff were most to blame in all this sad business; the preachers certainly took an over-active part.

Of the personal appearance of this "erroneous gentlewoman" we know nothing. I do not think, in spite of the presumptive evidence of the marked personal beauty of her descendants, that she was a handsome woman, else it would certainly be so stated. The author of the *Short Story of the Rise Reigne and Ruine of the Antinomians, Familists, and Libertines that infected the Churches of New England* calls her "a woman of a haughty and fierce carriage, of a nimble wit and active spirit, and a very voluble tongue, more bold than a man, though in understanding and judgment inferior to many women." He also termed her "the American Jezebel," and so did the traveller Josselyn in his *Account of Two Voyages to New England;* while Minister Hooker styled her "a wretched woman." Johnson, in his *Wonder-*

Working Providence, calls her the "master-piece of woman's wit." Governor Winthrop said she was "a woman of ready wit and bold spirit." Cotton Mather called her a virago, cunning, canting, and proud, but he did not know her.

We to-day can scarcely comprehend what these "double weekly lectures" must have been to these Boston women, with their extreme conscientiousness, their sombre religious belief, and their timid superstition, in their hard and perhaps homesick life. The materials for mental occupation and excitement were meagre; hence the spiritual excitement caused by Anne Hutchinson's prophesyings must have been to them a fascinating religious dissipation. Many were exalted with a supreme assurance of their salvation. Others, bewildered with spiritual doubts, fell into deep gloom and depression; and one woman in utter desperation attempted to commit a crime, and found therein a natural source of relief, saying "now she was sure she should be damned." Into all this doubt and depression the wives — to use Cotton Mather's phrase — "hooked in their husbands." So, perhaps, after all it was well to banish the fomenter of all these troubles and bewilderments.

Still, I wonder whether Anne Hutchinson's old neighbors and gossips did not regret these interesting meetings, these exciting prophesyings, when they were sternly ended. I hope they grieved for her when they heard of her cruel death by Indian massacre; and I know they remembered her unstinted, kindly offices in time of sickness and affliction; and I trust they honored "her ever sober and profitable carriage," and I suspect some of them in their inmost hearts deplored the Protestant Inquisition of their fathers and husbands, that caused her exile and consequent murder by the savages.

Samuel Johnson says, "As the faculty of writing is chiefly a masculine endowment, the reproach of making the world miserable has always been thrown upon women." As the faculty of literary composition at that day was wholly a masculine endowment, we shall never know what the Puritan women really thought of Anne Hutchinson, and whether they threw upon her any reproach.

We gain a slight knowledge of what Margaret Winthrop thought of all this religious ecstasy, this bitter quarrelling, from a letter written by her, and dated "Sad-Boston." She says : —

Sad thoughts possess my sperits, and I cannot repulce them ; wch makes me unfit for anythinge, wondringe what the Lord meanes by all these troubles among us. Shure I am that all shall worke to the best to them that love God, or rather are loved of hime, I know he will bring light out of obcurity and make his rituusnesse shine forth as clere as the nounday; yet I find in myself an aferce spiret, and a tremblinge hart, not so willing to submit to the will of God as I desyre. There is a time to plant, and a time to pull up that which is planted, which I could desyre might not be yet.

And so it would seem to us to-day that it was indeed a doubtful beginning to tear up with such violence even flaunting weeds, lest the tender and scattered grain, whose roots scarce held in the unfamiliar soil, might also be uprooted and wither and die. But the colony endured these trials, and flourished, as it did other trials, and still prospered.

Though written expression of their feelings is lacking, we know that the Boston neighbors gave to Anne Hutchinson that sincerest flattery — imitation. Perhaps her fellow-prophets should not be called imitators, but simply kindred religious spirits. The elements of society in colonial Boston were such as plentifully to produce and stimulate "disordered and heady persons."

Among them was Mary Dyer, thus described by Winthrop : —

The wife of William Dyer, a milliner in the New Exchange, a very proper and fair woman, notoriously infected with Mrs Hutchinsons errors, and very censorious and troublesome. She being of a very proud spirit and much addicted to revelations.

Another author called her "a comely grave woman, of a goodly personage, and of good report."

Some of these Boston neighbors lived to see two sad sights. Fair comely Mary Dyer, after a decade of unmolested and peaceful revelations in Rhode Island, returned to her early home, and persistently preached to her old friends, and then walked through Boston streets hand in hand with two young Quaker friends, condemned felons, to the sound of the drums of the train band, glorying in her companionship ; and then she was set on a gallows with a halter round her neck, while her two friends were hanged before her eyes; this was witnessed by such a multitude that the drawbridge broke under the weight of the returning North-enders. And six months later this very proper and fair woman herself was hanged in Boston, to rid the commonwealth of an intolerable plague.

A letter still exists, written by William Dyer to the Boston magistrates to "beg affectionately the life of my deare wife." It is most touching, most heart-rending; it ends thus, "Yourselves have been husbands of wife or wives, and so am I, yea to one most dearlye beloved. Oh do not you deprive me of her, but I pray you give me her out againe. Pitye me — I beg it with teares."

The tears still stain this poor sorrowful, appealing letter, — a missive so gentle, so timid, so full of affection, of grief, that I cannot now read it unmoved and I do indeed "pitye" thee. William Dyer's tears have not been the only ones to fall on his beautiful, tender words.

Another interesting neighbor living where Washington Street crossed Brattle Street was the bride, young Madam Bellingham, whose

marriage had caused such a scandal in good
society in Boston. Winthrop's account of
this affair is the best that could be given : —

The governour Mr Bellingham was married.
The young gentlewoman was ready to be contracted to a friend of his who lodged in his
house, and by his consent had proceeded so far
with her, when on a sudden the governour treated
with her, and obtained her for himself. He
excused it by the strength of his affection, and
that she was not absolutely promised to the
other gentleman. Two errors more he committed upon it. 1. That he would not have his
contract published where he dwelt, contrary to
the order of court. 2. That he married himself
contrary to the constant practice of the country.
The great inquest prosecuted him for breach of
the order of the court, and at the court following
in the fourth month, the secretary called him to
answer the prosecution. But he not going off
the bench, as the manner was, and but few of the
magistrates present, he put it off to another time,
intending to speak with him privately, and with
the rest of the magistrates about the case, and
accordingly he told him the reason why he did
not proceed, viz., that being unwilling to command him publicly to go off the bench, and yet
not thinking it fit he should sit as a judge, when

he was by law to answer as an offender. This he took ill, and said he would not go off the bench except he were commanded.

I think the young English girl, Penelope Pelham, must have been sadly bewildered by the strange abrupt ways of the new land, by her dictatorial elderly lover, by his autocratic and singular marriage with her, by the attempted action of the government against him. She had a long life thereafter, for he lived to be eighty years old, and she survived him thirty years.

A very querulous and turbulent neighbor who lived on Milk Street was Mistress Ann Hibbins, the wife of one of Boston's honored citizens. Her husband had been unsuccessful in business matters, and this "so discomposed his wife's spirit that she was scarce ever well settled in her mind afterwards," and at last was put out of the church and by her strange carriage gave occasion to her superstitious neighbors to charge her with being a witch. She was brought to trial for witchcraft, convicted, sentenced, and hung upon a Thursday lecture day, in spite of her social position, and the fact that her brother was Governor Bellingham. She had other friends, high in authority, as her will shows, and she had the belongings of a colonial dame, " a diamond ring, a taffety cloke, silk gown and kirtle, pinck-colored pet-ticoat, and money in the deske." Minister Beach wrote to Increase Mather in 1684: —

I have sometimes told you your famous Mr Norton once said at his own table before Mr Wilson, Elder Penn and myself and wife who had the honour to be his guests — that the wife of one of your magistrates, I remember, was hanged for a witch only for having more wit than her neighbors. It was his very expression; she having as he explained it, unhappily guessed that two of her prosecutors, whom she saw talk-ing in the street were talking about her — which cost her her life, notwithstanding all he could do to the contrary.

It would naturally be thought, from the affectionate and intense devotion of the colonists to the school which had just be-come " Harvard-Colledge," that Mr. Nathan-iel Eaton, the head-master of the freshly established seat of learning, would be a citi-zen of much esteem, and his wife a dame of as dignified carriage and honored station as any of her Boston and Cambridge neighbors.

Let us see whether such was the case. Mr. Eaton had had much encouragement to continue at the head of the college for life; he had been offered a tract of five hundred acres of land, and liberal support had been offered by the government, and he "had many scholars, the sons of gentlemen and of others of best note in the country." Yet when he fell out with one of his ushers on very slight occasion, he struck the usher and caused two more to hold the poor fellow while he beat him two hundred stripes with a heavy walnut cudgel; and when poor Usher Briscoe fell a-praying, in fear of dying, Master Eaton beat him further for taking the name of God in vain. When all this cruelty was laid to him in open court "his answers were full of pride and disdain," and he said he had this unvarying rule, "that he would not give over correcting till he had subdued the party to his will." And upon being questioned about other malpractices, especially the ill and scant diet provided by him for the students, though good board had been paid by them, he, Adam-like, "put it off to his wife."

Her confession of her connection with the

matter is still in existence, and proves her accomplishments as a generous and tidy housewife about equal to his dignity and lenity as head of the college. It is a most curious and minute document, showing what her duties were, and the way she performed them, and also giving an interesting glimpse of college life in those days. It reads thus : —

For their breakfast that it was not so well ordered, the flower not so fine as it might, nor so well boiled or stirred at all times that it was so, it was my sin of neglect, and want of care that ought to have been in one that the Lord had intrusted with such a work.

Concerning their beef, that was allowed them, as they affirm, which I confess had been my duty to have seen they should have had it, and continued to have had it, because it was my husbands command ; but truly I must confess, to my shame, I cannot remember that ever they had it nor that ever it was taken from them.

And that they had not so good or so much provision in my husbands absence as presence, I conceive it was, because he would call sometimes for butter or cheese when I conceived there was no need of it ; yet for as much as the scholars did otherways apprehend, I desire to see the evil that was in the carriage of that as in the other and to take shame to myself for it.

And that they sent down for more, when they had not enough, and the maid should answer, if they had not, they should not. I must confess that I have denied them cheese, when they have sent for it, and it have been in the house, for which I shall humbly beg pardon to them, and own the shame, and confess my sin.

And for such provoking words which my servants have given, I cannot own them, but am sorry any such should be given in my house.

And for bad fish, they had it brought to table, I am sorry there was that cause of offence given; I acknowledge my sin in it. . . . I am much ashamed it should be in the family, and not prevented by myself or my servants, and I humbly acknowledge my negligence in it.

And that they made their beds at any time, were my straits never so great, I am sorry they were ever put to it.

For the Moor, his lying in Sam Hough's sheet and pillow-bier, it hath a truth in it; he did so at one time and it gave Sam Hough just cause for offence; and that it was not prevented by my care and watchfulness I desire to take the shame and the sorrow for it.

And that they eat the Moor's crusts, and the swine and they had share and share alike; and the Moor to have beer, and they denied it, and if they had not enough, for my maid to answer they should not, I am an utter stranger to these things, and know not the least foot-steps for them so to charge me; and if my servants were guilty of such miscarriages, had the boarders complained of it unto myself, I should have thought it my sin, if I had not sharply removed my servants and endeavored reform.

And for bread made of sour heated meal, though I know of but once that it was so since I kept house, yet John Wilson affirms that it was twice; and I am truly sorry that any of it was spent amongst them.

For beer and bread that it was denied them by me betwixt meals, truly I do not remember, that ever I did deny it unto them; and John Wilson will affirm that, generally, the bread and beer was free for the boarders to go to.

And that money was demanded of them for washing the linen, tis true that it was propounded to them but never imposed upon them.

And for their pudding being given the last day of the week without butter or suet, and that I said, it was a miln of Manchester in old England, its true that I did say so, and am sorry, that had any cause of offence given them by having it so.

And for their wanting beer betwixt brewings, a

week or half a week together, I am sorry that it was so at any time, and should tremble to have it so, were it in my hands to do again.

And whereas they say, that sometimes they have sent down for more meat and it hath been denied, when it have been in the house, I must confess, to my shame, that I have denied them oft, when they have sent for it, and it have been in the house.

Truly a pitiful tale of shiftless stinginess, of attempted extortion, of ill-regulated service, and of overworked housewifery as well.

The Reverend Mr. Eaton did not escape punishment for his sins. After much obstinacy he "made a very solid, wise, eloquent, and serious confession, condemning himself in all particulars." The court, with Winthrop at the head, bore lightly upon him after this confession, and yet when sentence of banishment from the college, and restriction from teaching within the jurisdiction, was passed, and he was fined £30, he did not give glory to God as was expected, but turned away with a discontented look. Then the church took the matter up to discipline him, and the schoolmaster promptly ran away, leaving debts of a thousand pounds.

The last scene in the life of Mrs. Eaton may be given in Winthrop's words : —

Mr. Nathaniel Eaton being come to Virginia, took upon him to be a minister there, but was given up to extreme pride and sensuality, being usually drunken, as the custom is there. He sent for his wife and children. Her friends here persuaded her to stay awhile, but she went, notwithstanding, and the vessel was never heard of after.

So you see she had friends and neighbors who wished her to remain in New England with them, and who may have loved her in spite of the sour bread, and scant beer, and bad fish, that she doled out to the college students.

There was one visitor who flashed upon this chill New England scene like a brilliant tropical bird ; with all the subtle fascination of a foreigner ; speaking a strange language ; believing a wicked Popish faith ; and englamoured with the romance of past adventure, with the excitement of incipient war. This was Madam La Tour, the young wife of one of the rival French governors of Acadia. The relations of Massachusetts, of Boston town, to the quarrels of these two ambi-

tious and unscrupulous Frenchmen, La Tour
and D'Aulnay, form one of the most curious
and interesting episodes in the history of the
colony.

Many unpleasant and harassing complica-
tions and annoyances had arisen between the
French and English colonists, in the more
northern plantations, when, in 1643, in June,
Governor La Tour surprised his English
neighbors by landing in Boston " with two
friars and two women sent to wait upon La
Tour His Lady " — and strange sights they
truly were in Boston. He came ashore at
Governor Winthrop's garden (now Fort Winthrop), and his arrival was heralded by a
frightened woman, one Mrs. Gibbons, who
chanced to be sailing in the bay, and saw the
approach of the French boat, and hastened
to warn the Governor. Perhaps Mrs. Gibbons had a premonitory warning of the
twenty-five hundred pounds her husband
was to lose at a later date through his confidence in the persuasive Frenchman. Governor and Madam Winthrop and their two
sons and a daughter-in-law were sitting in
the Governor's garden in the summer sunshine, and though thoroughly surprised, they

greeted the unexpected visitor, La Tour, with civilities, and escorted him to Boston town, not without some internal tremors and much deep mortification of the Governor when he thought of the weakness and poverty of Boston, with Castle Island deserted, as was plainly shown to the foreigner by the lack of any response to his salute of guns; and the inference was quick to come that the Frenchman "might have spoiled Boston."

But La Tour's visit was most friendly; all he wished was free mercature and the coöperation of the English colony. And he desired to land his men for a short time, that they might refresh themselves after their long voyage; "so they landed in small companies that our women might not be affrighted with them." And the Governor dined the French officers, and the New England warriors of the train-band entertained the visiting Gallic soldiers, and they exercised and trained before each other, all in true Boston hospitable fashion, as is the custom to this day. And the Governor bourgeoned with as much of an air of importance as possible, "being regularly attended with a good guard of halberts and musketeers;" and thus tried to live down

the undignified heralding of a fellow-governor
by a badly scared woman neighbor. And the
cunning Frenchman, as did another of his
race, "with sugared words sought to addulce
all matters." He flattered the sober Boston
magistrates, and praised everything about
the Boston army, and " showed much admiration professing he could not have believed it,
if he had not seen it." And the foreigners
were so well treated (though Winthrop was
blamed afterwards by stern Endicott and the
Rome-hating ministers) that they came again
the following summer, when La Tour asked
material assistance. He received it, and he
lingered till autumn, and barely eight days
after he left, Madam La Tour landed in Boston from London ; and strange and sad must
the little town have seemed to her after her
past life. She was in a state of much anger,
and at once brought suit against the master
of the ship for not carrying her and her belongings to the promised harbor in Acadia ;
for trading on the way until she nearly fell
into the hands of her husband's enemy,
D'Aulnay. The merchants of Charlestown
and Salem sided with the ship's captain.
The solid men of Boston gallantly upheld

and assisted the lady. The jury awarded her two thousand pounds damages, and bitterly did one of the jury — Governor Winthrop's son — suffer for it, for he was afterwards arrested in London, and had to give bond for four thousand pounds to answer to a suit in the Court of Admiralty about the Boston decision in favor of the Lady La Tour.

In the mean time ambassadors from the rival Acadian governor, D'Aulnay, arrived in New England, and were treated with much honor and consideration by the diplomatic Boston magistrates. I think I can read between the lines that the Bostonians really liked La Tour, who must have had much personal attraction and magnetism; but they feared D'Aulnay, who had brought against the Massachusetts government a claim of eight thousand pounds damages. The Governor sent to D'Aulnay a propitiatory gift of "a very fair new sedan chair (of no use to us)," and I should fancy scarcely of much more use in Acadia; and which proved a very cheap way of staving off paying the eight thousand pounds.

Madam La Tour sailed off at last with three laden ships to her husband, in spite of D'Aulnay's dictum that "she was known to be the cause of all her husband's contempt and rebellion, and therefore they could not let her go to him." La Tour's stronghold was captured shortly after "by assault and scalado" when he was absent, and his jewels, plate, and furniture to the amount of ten thousand pounds were seized, and his wife too; and she died in three weeks, of a broken heart, and "her little child and gentlewomen were sent to France."

I think these Boston neighbors were entitled to a little harmless though exciting gossip two or three years later, when they learned that after D'Aulnay's death the fascinating widower La Tour had promptly married Widow D'Aulnay, thus regaining his jewels and plate, and both had settled down to a long and peaceful life in Nova Scotia.

CHAPTER V.

A FEARFULL FEMALE TRAVAILLER.

IN the autumn and winter of the year
1704, Madam Sarah Knight, a resident
of Boston, made a journey on horseback
from Boston to New York, and returned in
the same manner. It was a journey difficult
and perilous, "full of buggbears to a fearfull
female travailler," and which "startled a
masculine courage," but which was performed by this woman with the company
and protection only of hired guides, the
"Western Post," or whatever chance traveller she might find journeying her way, at
a time when brave men feared to travel
through New England, and asked for public
prayers in church before starting on a journey of twenty miles. She was probably the
first woman who made such a journey, in
such a manner, in this country.

Madam Knight was the daughter of Captain Kemble, of Boston, who was in 1656 set

two hours in the public stocks as a punishment for his "lewd and unseemly behavior," which consisted in his kissing his wife "publicquely" on the Sabbath Day, upon the doorstep of his house, when he had just returned from a voyage and absence of three years.

The diary which Madam kept on this eventful trip contains the names of no persons of great historical interest, though many of historical mention; but it is such a vivacious and sprightly picture of the customs of the time, and such a valuable description of localities as they then appeared, that it has an historical interest of its own, and is a welcome addition to the few diaries and records of the times which we possess.

Everything was not all serene and pleasant in the years 1704 and 1705 in New England. Events had occurred which could not have been cheerful for Madam Knight to think of when riding through the lonely Narragansett woods and along the shores of the Sound. News of the frightful Indian massacre at Deerfield had chilled the very hearts of the colonists. At Northampton shocking and most unexpected cruelties had been perpetrated by the red men. At Lancaster, not any too far from Boston, the Indians had been most obstreperous. We can imagine Madam Knight had no very pleasant thoughts of these horrors when she wrote her description of the red men whom she saw in such numbers in Connecticut. Bears and wolves, too, abounded in the lonely woods of Massachusetts and Connecticut. The howls of wolves were heard every night, and rewards were paid by New England towns for the heads of wolves that were killed, provided the heads were brought into town and nailed to the side of the meeting-house. Twenty-one years later than Madam Knight's journey, in 1725, twenty bears were killed in one week in September, within two miles of Boston, so says the *History of Roxbury;* and all through the eighteenth century bears were hunted and killed in upper Narragansett. Hence "buggbears" were not the only bears to be dreaded on the lonely journey.

The year 1704 was memorable also because it gave birth to the first newspaper in the colonies, the *Boston News-Letter.* Only a few copies were printed each week, and each copy contained but four or five square feet of print, and the first number contained but one advertisement — that of the man who printed it.

When Madam Knight's journal was published in New York by Mr. Theodore Dwight, in 1825, the editor knew nothing of the diarist, not even her family name; hence it was confidently believed by many that the journal was merely a clever and entertaining fiction. In 1852, however, Miss Caulkins published her history of the town of New London, and contradicted that belief, for she gave an account of the last days of Madam Knight, which were spent in Norwich and New London. Madam Knight's daughter married the Colonel Livingston who is mentioned in the journal, and left no children. From a descendant of Mrs. Livingston's administratrix, Mrs. Christopher, the manuscript of the journal was obtained for publication in 1825, it having been carefully preserved all those years. In *Blackwood's Magazine* for the same year an article appeared, entitled *Travelling in America*, which reprinted nearly all of Madam Knight's journal, and which showed a high appreciation of its literary and historical merits. In 1858 it was again printed by request in *Littell's Living Age*, with some notes of Madam Knight's life, chiefly compiled from Miss Caulkins' *History of New London*, and again provoked much inquiry and discussion. Recently a large portion of the journal has been reprinted in the *Library of American Literature*, with many alterations, however, in the spelling, use of capitals, and punctuation, thus detracting much from the interest and quaintness of the work; and most unnecessarily, since it is perfectly easy to read and understand it as first printed, when, as the editor said, "the original orthography was carefully preserved for fear of introducing any unwarrantable modernism."

The first edition is now seldom seen for sale, and being rare is consequently high-priced. The little shabby, salmon-colored copy of the book which I saw was made interesting by two manuscript accounts of Sarah Knight, which were inserted at the end of the book, and which are very valuable, since they give positive proof of the reality of the fair traveller, as well as additional facts of her life.

The first account was in a fine old-fashioned, unpunctuated handwriting, on yellow, time-stained paper, and read thus : —

Madam Knight was born in Boston She was the daughter of Capt. Kemble who was a rich merchant of Boston he was a native of Great Britain settled in Boston built him a large house for that day near New North Square in the year 1676 this daughter Sarah Kemble was married to a son of a London trader by the name of Knight he died abroad and left her a smart young widow in October 1703 she made a journey to New York to claim some property of his there. She returned on horse-backe March 1705 Soon after her return she opened a school for children Dr. Frankelin and Dr Saml Mather secured their first rudiments of Education from her her parents both died and as She was the only child they left she continued to keep school in the Mansion house till the year 1714. She then sold the estate to Peter Papillion he died not long after in the year 1736 Thomas Hutchinson Esqr purchased the estate of John Wolcott, who was administrator of the Papillion estate Mr Hutchinson gave the estate to his daughter Hannah who was the wife of Dr Saml Mather. The force of Madam Knight's Diamond Ring was displayed on several panes of glass in the old

house in the year 1763 Dr Mather had the house
new glazed and one pane of glass was preserved
as a curiosity for years till 1775 it was lost at the
conflagration when Charlestown was burnt by
the British June 17th. The lines on the pane of
glass were committed to memory by the present
writer. She was an original genius our ideas of
Madam are formed from hearing Dr Frankelin
and Dr Mather converse about their old school
misstress

> Through many toils and many frights
> I have returned poor Sarah Knights
> Over great rocks and many stones
> God has preserv'd from fractur'd bones

as spelt on the pane of glass.

Underneath this account was written in
the clear, distinct chirography of Isaiah
Thomas, the veteran printer, this endorse-
ment : —

The above was written by Mrs. Hannabell
Crocker, of Boston, granddaughter of the Rev.
Cotton Mather, and presented to me by that
lady. — ISAIAH THOMAS.

The other manuscript account is substan-
tially the same, though in a different handwriting ; it tells of the pane of glass with the
rhymed inscription being "preserved as a
curiosity by an antiquicrity" (which is a

delightful and useful old word-concoction), "until the British set fire to the town," in Revolutionary times, and "Poor Madam Knight's poetrys, with other curiosities, were consumed." It says, "She obtained the honorable title of Madam by being a famous schoolmistress in her day. She taught Dr. Franklin to write. She was highly respected by Dr. Cotton Mather as a woman of good wit & pleasant humour."

Sarah Knight was born in 1666, and thus was about thirty-eight years old when she made her "perilous journey." She started October 2d, and did not reach New York until December 6th. Of course much of this time was spent visiting friends and kinsfolk in New London and New Haven, and often, too, she had to wait to obtain companion travellers. She rode upon the first night of her journey until very late in order to "overtake the post," and this is the account of her reception at her first lodging-place : —

My guide dismounted and very complasently and shewed the door signing to me with his hand to Go in, which I Gladly did. But had not gone many steps into the room ere I was interrogated

by a young Lady I understood afterwards was
the Eldest daughter of the family, with these,
or words to this purpose, (viz) Law for mee —
what in the world brings you here at this time-a-
night? I never see a woman on the Rode so
Dreadfull late in all my Varsall Life. Who are
You? Where are you going? I 'm scar'd out of
my witts — with much now of the same Kind
I stood aghast Prepareing no reply — when in
come my Guide — to him Madam turn'd roreing
out : Lawfull heart John is it You? how de do?
Where in the world are you going with this woman? Who is She? John made no Ans'r but
sat down in the corner, fumbled out his black
Junk, and saluted that instead of Debb. She
then turned agen to mee and fell anew into her
silly questions without asking mee to sit down.
I told her she treated mee very Rudely and I did
not think it my duty to answer her unmannerly
Questions. But to gett ridd of them I told her
I come there to have the Posts company with
me to-morrow on my Journey &c. Miss stared
awhile, drew a chair bid me sitt And then run
upstairs and putts on two or three Rings (or else
I had not seen them before) and returning sett
herself just before me shewing the way to Red-
ing, that I might see her Ornaments.

It appears from this account that human

nature, or rather feminine love of display, was the same in colonial times as in the present day.

Very vivid are her descriptions of the various beds upon which she reposed. This is her entry in her diary after the first night of her journey : —

I pray'd Miss to shew me where I must Lodg. Shee conducted me to a parlour in a little back Lento, which was almost filled with the bedstead, which was so high that I was forced to climb on a chair to gitt up to ye wretched bed that lay on it, on which having Strecht my tired Limbs, and lay'd my head on a Sad-colour'd pillow, I began to think on the transactions of ye past day.

We can imagine her (if such an intrusive fancy is not impertinent after one hundred and eighty years), attired in her night-hood and her "flowered calico night-rayle with high collared neck," climbing wearily upon a chair and thence to the mountainous bed with its dingy pillow. The fashion of wearing "immoderate great rayles" had been prohibited by law in Massachusetts in 1634, but the garment mentioned must have been some kind of a loose gown worn in the day-

time, for we cannot fancy that even the meddlesome interference and aspiring ambition
for omnipotence of those Puritan magistrates
would make them dare to attempt to con-
trol what kind of a nightgown a woman
should wear.

Here is another vivid description of a
night's lodging, where her room was shared,
as was the country custom of that time (and
indeed for many years later), by the men
who had journeyed with her : —

Arriving at my apartment found it to be a
little Lento Chamber furnished amongst other
Rubbish with a High Bedd and a Low one, a
Long Table, a Bench and a Bottomless chair.
Little Miss went to scratch up my Kennell
which Russelled as if shee 'd bin in the Barn
amongst the Husks, and supose such was the
contents of the tickin — nevertheless being exceeding weary-down I laid my poor Carkes
(never more tired) and found my Covering as
scanty as my Bed was hard. Anon I heard another Russelling noise in Ye Room — called to
know the matter — Little Miss said shee was
making a bed for the men ; who, when they were
in Bed complained their leggs lay out of it by
reason of its shortness — my poor bones complained bitterly not being used to such Lodgings,

and so did the man who was with us ; and poor
I made but one Grone, which was from the time
I went to bed to the time I Riss, which was
about three in the morning, Setting up by the
Fire till Light.

The word "lento," or "lean to," was sometimes called "linter," and you will still hear
old-fashioned or aged country-people use the
word. The "lean-to" was the rear portion
of a form of house peculiar to New England,
which was two stories high in front, with a
roof which sloped down from a steep gable
to a very low single story at the rear.

Madam Sarah speaks with some surprise
throughout her travels of the height of the
beds, so it is evident that very towering beds
were not in high fashion in Boston in 1704,
in spite of the exceeding tall four-posters
that have descended to us from our ancestors,
and which surely no one could mount in modern days without a chair as an accessory.
Even a chair was not always a sufficient
stepping-block by the bedsides that Madam
Sarah found, for she thus writes : "He invited us to his house, and shewed me two
pair of stairs, viz, one up the loft, and tother
up the Bedd, which was as hard as it was

high, and warmed with a hott stone at the foot."

After the good old Puritan custom of contumelious reviling, in which clergymen, laymen, and legal lights alike joined, Madam Knight could show a rare choice of epithets and great fluency of uncomplimentary description when angered. Having expected to lodge at the house of a Mr. DeVille in Narragansett, and being refused, she writes thus of the DeVilles : —

I questioned whether we ought to go to the Devil to be helpt out of the affliction. However, like the Rest of Deluded souls that post to ye Infernall denn, Wee made all possible speed to this Devil's Habitation ; where alliting, in full assurance of good accommodation, wee were going in. But meeting his two daughters, as I suposed twins, they so neerly resembled each other both in features and habit and look't as old as the Divel himself, and quite as Ugly. We desired entertainment, but could hardly get a word out of 'um, till with our Importunity telling them our necessity &c they call'd the old Sophister, who was as sparing of his words as his daughters had bin, and no or none, was the reply's he made us to our demands. Hee differed only in this from the old fellow in tother Country, hee let us depart. However I thought it proper to warn poor Travaillers to endeavour to Avoid falling into circumstances like ours, which at our next Stage I sat down and did as followeth : —

> May all that dread the cruel fiend of night
> Keep on and not at this curst Mansion light
> Tis Hell : Tis Hell : and Devills here do dwell
> Here Dwells the Devill — surely this is Hell.
> Nothing but Wants : a drop to cool yo're Tongue
> Cant be procured those cruel Fiends among
> Plenty of horrid grins and looks sevear
> Hunger and thirst, But pitty's banish'd here.
> The Right hand keep, if Hell on Earth you fear —

Madam Knight had a habit of "dropping into poetry" very readily and upon almost any subject. Upon the moon, upon poverty, even upon the noise of drunken topers in the next room to her own. The night-scene that brought forth the rhymes upon rum was graced by a conversation upon the derivation of the word Narragansett, and her report of it is of much interest, and is always placed among the many and various authorities for, and suggestions about, the meaning of the word : —

I went to bed which tho' pretty hard Yet neet

and handsome but I could get no sleep because
of the Clamor of some of the Town-tope-ers in
next Room who were entered into a strong de-
bate concerning ye Signifycation of the name of
their Country (viz) Narraganset. One said it was
named so by ye Indians because there grew a
Brier there of a prodigious Highth and bigness,
the like hardly ever known, called by the Indians
Narragansett. And quotes an Indian of so Bar-
berous a name for his Author that I could not
write it. His Antagonist Replyd No. — It was
from a spring it had its name, which he well knew
where it was, which was extreem cold in summer,
and as Hott as could be imagined in the winter
which was much resorted to by the natives and
by them called Narragansett (Hott & Cold) and
that was the originall of their places name —
with a thousand Impertinances not worth notice,
which He uttered with such a Roreing voice &
Thundering blows with the fist of wickedness on
the Table that it pierced my very head. I heart-
ily fretted and wisht 'um tonguetyed; but with
little success.

They kept calling for tother Gill which while
they were swallowing, was some Intermission But
presently like Oyle to fire encreased the flame.
I set my Candle on a Chest by the bedside, and
setting up fell to my old way of composing my
Resentments in the following manner : —

> I ask thy aid O Potent Rum
> To charm these wrangling Topers Dum
> Thou hast their Giddy Brains possest
> The man confounded with the Beast
> And I, poor I, can get no rest
> Intoxicate them with thy fumes
> O still their Tongues till morning comes

And I know not but my wishes took effect for the dispute soon ended with tother Dram.

To one who, unused to venturing abroad in boats on stormy waters, has trusted her bodily safety to one of those ticklish Indian vehicles, a canoe, this vivid account of the sensations of an early female colonist in a similar situation may prove of interest; nor do I think, after the lapse of centuries, could the description be improved by the added words of our newer and more profuse vocabulary : —

The Cannoo was very small & shallow so that when we were in she seemd redy to take in water which greatly terrify'd me, and caused me to be very circumspect, sitting with my hands fast on each side, my eyes stedy, not daring so much as to lodge my tongue a hairs breadth more on one side of my mouth than tother, nor so much as think on Lotts wife, for a very thought would have oversett our wherey.

We are so accustomed to hearing of the great veneration and respect always shown in olden times by children toward their parents, and the dignified reserve and absolute authority of parents towards children, that the following scene rather shocks our established notions : —

Thursday about 3 in the afternoon I set forward with neighbour Polly & Jemima a girl about 18 years old, who her father said he had been to fetch out of the Narragansetts and said they had rode thirty miles that day on a sorry lean Jade with only a Bagg under her for a pillion which the poor Girl often complain'd was very uneasy. Wee made Good speed along wch made poor Jemima make many a sowr face the mare being a very hard trotter, and after many a hearty & bitter Oh she at length low'd out: Lawful Heart father ! this bare mare hurts mee Dingeely. I'm direfull sore I vow, with many words to that purpose. Poor Child — sais Gaffer — she us't to serve your mother so. I dont care how mother ust to do, quoth Jemima in a passionate tone. At which the old man Laught and kikt his Jade o' the side, which made her Jolt ten times harder. About seven that evening we came to New London Ferry here by reason of a very high wind, we mett with great difficulty in getting over. The

boat tost exceedingly and our Horses cappered
at a very Surprising rate and set us all in a fright
especially poor Jemima who desired father to say
So Jack! to the Jade to make her stand.   But
the careless parent, taking no notice of her
repeated desires, She Rored out in a Pasionate
manner Pray Suth father Are you deaf?   Say So
Jack to the Jade I tell you.   The Dutiful Parent
obeyed saying So Jack So Jack as gravely as if
he had bin saying Chatchise after young Miss
who with her fright look't all the Colours of ye
Rainbow.

It is very evident from entries in her Journal that Madam Knight thought much of
gratifying her appetite, for the food she obtained at her different resting-places is often
described.   She says : —

Landlady told us shee had some mutton which
shee would broil.   In a little time she bro't it in
but it being pickled and my Guide said it smelt
strong of head-sause we left it and paid six pence
apiece for our dinners which was only smell.

Again, she thus describes a meal : —

Having call'd for something to eat the woman
bro't in a Twisted thing like a cable, but something whiter, laying it on the bord, tugg'd for
life to bring it into a capacity to spread ; which

having with great pains accomplished shee served
a dish of Pork and Cabage I supose the remains
of Dinner. The sause was of a deep purple
which I tho't was boiled in her dye Kettle ; the
bread was Indian and everything on the Table
service agreeable to these. I being hungry gott
a little down, but my stomach was soon cloy'd
and what cabage I swallowed served me for a
Cudd the whole day after.

The early colonists never turned very readily to Indian meal and pumpkins — pumpions
as they called them in the "times wherein
old Pompion was a saint;" and Johnson,
in his *Wonder-Working Providence*, reproved
them for making a jest of pumpkins, since
they were so good a food. Madam Knight
had them offered to her very often, " pumpkin sause" and "pumpkin bred." "We
would have eat a morsell ourselves But the
Pumpkin and Indian-mixt Bread had such an
aspect, and the Bare-legg'd Punch so awkerd
or rather Awfull a sound that we left both."

She gives a glimpse of rather awkward
table-manners when she complains that in
Connecticut masters permitted their slaves
to sit and eat with them, "and into the dish
goes the black Hoof as freely as the white

hand." Doubtless in those comparatively forkless days fingers were very freely used at the table.

She tells many curious facts about Connecticut. Divorces were plentiful in that State, as they are at the present day. She writes : —

These uncomely Standaways are too much in Vogue among the English in this Indulgent Colony as their Records plentifully prove, and that on very trivial matters of which some have been told me, but are not Proper to be Related by a Female Pen.

She says they will not allow harmless kissing among the young people, and she tells of a curious custom at weddings, where the bridegroom ran away and had to be chased and dragged back by force to the bride.

Her descriptions of the city of New York; of the public vendues "where they give drinks;" of the Dutch houses and women; of the "sley-riding" where she "mett fifty or sixty sleys," are all very entertaining. There were few sleighs in Boston at that date. Everything is compared with "ours in Boston," or said to be "not like Boston," after a fashion still somewhat

followed by the Boston "Female Pen" of
the present day. As New York then was
only a small town of five thousand inhabitants, while Big Boston possessed ten thousand inhabitants, such comparisons were
certainly justifiable.

We must give her vivid and vivacious
picture of a country "lubber" in a merchant's shop :—

In comes a tall country fellow with his Alfo-
geos full of Tobaco. He advanced to the middle
of the room, makes an awkward nodd and spit-
ting a large deal of Aromatic Tincture, he gave
a scrape with his shovel-like shoo, leaving a small
shovel-full of dirt on the floor, made a full stop,
hugging his own pretty body with his hands
under his arms, Stood Staring round him like a
Catt let out of a Baskett. At last like the creature Balaam rode on he opened his mouth and
said *Have you any Ribinen for Hat bands to sell I
pray?* The Questions and answers about the
pay being past the Ribin is bro't and opened.
Bumpkin simpers, cryes, *Its confounded Gay I
vow;* and beckoning to the door in comes Joan
Tawdry, dropping about 50 curtsies, and stands
by him. He shews her the Ribin. *Law You,*
sais shee, *its right Gent, do you take it, its dread-
ful pretty.* Then she enquires : *Have you any*

hood silk I pray? which being brought and bought. *Have you any Thred silk to sew it with?* says shee, which being accomodated with they departed.

Though Madam Knight left no account of the costume which she wore on her "perilous journey," we know very well what the fashions of the time were and of what her dress consisted. She wore a woollen round-gown, perhaps of camlet, perhaps of calimanco, of which the puffed sleeves came to the elbow and were finished with knots of ribbons and ruffles. Riding-habits were then never worn. I am sure she did not wear a neck-ruff on this journey, but a scarf or neck-kerchief or "cross cloth" instead. Long gloves of leather or kid protected her fair hands, and came to the elbow, and were firmly secured at the top by "glove-tightens" made of braided black horsehair. A pointed beaver or beaverette hat covered her head; the hat and peruke had not then reached the excessive size which made them for a lady's "riding equipage" so bitterly and openly condemned in 1737 as an exceeding and abominable affectation. She doubtless wore instead of the fine, stately peruke, a cap, a "round cap," which did not cover the ears, or a "strap cap," which came under the chin ; or perhaps a "quoif" or a "ciffer"—New England French for *coiffure*. During her cold winter ride home she surely donned a hood. One is described at that date thus : "A woman's worsted camlet riding-hood of grayish color faced with crimson coulour'd Persian." Over her shoulders she wore a heavy woollen short cloak, or a scarlet "whittle," and doubtless also added a "drugget-petticoat" for warmth, or a "safeguard" for protection against mud. High-heeled pointed shoes of leather, with knots of green ribbon or silver buckles, completed Madam Sarah's picturesque and comfortable attire. One other useful article of dress, or rather of protection, she surely as a lady of high gentility carried and wore : a riding-mask made of black velvet with a silver mouthpiece, or with two little strings with a silver bead at the end, which she placed in either corner of her mouth, to hold her mask firmly in place.

The "nagg" upon which Madam rode was without doubt a pacer, as were all good saddle-horses at that date. No one making any pretension to fashion or good style would ride upon a trotting-horse, nor indeed until Revolutionary times was a trotter regarded as of any account or worth.

I do not think Madam Knight had a Narragansett pacer, for as soon as they were raised in any numbers they were sent at once to the West Indies for the use of the wives and daughters of the wealthy sugar-planters, and few New England people could afford to own them. The " horse furniture " of which she speaks included, of course, her side-saddle and saddle-bag, which held her travelling-wardrobe and her precious journal.

Madam Sarah Knight did not end her days in Boston. She removed to Norwich, Conn., and in 1717 it is recorded that she gave a silver cup for the communion-service of the church there. The town in gratitude, by vote, gave her liberty to " sitt in the pue where she was used to sitt in ye meeting house." She also kept an inn on the Livingston Farm near New London, and I doubt not a woman of her large experience kept a good ordinary. No rustling beds, no sad-colored pillow-bears, no saucy maids, no noisy midnight topers, no doubtful fricassees, no pumpkin-bread, and, above all, no bare-legged punch in her house.

It is painful to record, however, that in 1718 the teacher of Benjamin Franklin and friend of Cotton Mather was indicted and fined for "selling strong liquor to Indians."

Altogether, Madam Knight was far ahead of the time in which she lived. She was a woman of great energy and talent. She kept a school when a woman-teacher was almost unheard of. She ran a tavern, a shop. She wrote poetry and a diary. She cultivated a farm, and owned mills, and speculated largely in Indian lands, and was altogether a sharp business-woman ; and she must have been counted an extraordinary character in those early days.

CHAPTER VI.

TWO COLONIAL ADVENTURESSES.

A "STRANGE true story of Louisiana" so furnished with every attractive element of romance, so calculated to satisfy every exaction of literary art, that it seems marvellous it has not been eagerly seized upon and frequently utilized by dramatists and novelists, is that of a Louisiana princess — or pretender — whose death in a Parisian convent in 1771 furnished a fruitful topic of speculation and conversation in the courts of France, Austria, Russia, and Prussia. This Louisiana princess (were she no pretender) was the daughter-in-law of Peter the Great of Russia, wife of the Grand Duke Alexis, and mother of Peter II. of Russia. The story, as gathered from a few European authorities and some old French chronicles and histories of Louisiana, is this.

The Princess Christine, daughter of a German princeling and wife of the Grand Duke

Alexis, is said by Russian official and historical records to have died in 1716 after a short
and most unhappy married life with a brutal
royal profligate, and to have been buried
with proper court honors and attendance.
But there is another statement, half-history,
half-romance, which denies that she died at
that time, and asserts that her death and
burial were but a carefully planned deception, to permit her to escape her intolerable
life in Russia, and only concealed her successful flight from St. Petersburg and the
power of the Russian throne. Aided by the
famous Countess Königsmark, the princess,
after some delay and frightened hiding in
France, sailed from the port of L'Orient,
accompanied by an old devoted court re-
tainer named Walter. Of course there must
always be a lover to form a true romance,
and a young officer named D'Aubant successfully fills that rôle. He had often seen
Christine in the Russian court, and had
rescued her from danger when she was hunting in the Hartz Mountains, and had cherished
for her a deep though hopeless love. When
the news of her death came to the knowledge of Chevalier D'Aubant, he sadly left

the Czar's service and went to France. Soon after he chanced to see at the cathedral in Poitiers a woman who raised her veil, glanced at him with a look of recognition, and apparently a face like that of his loved Christine. After long search for the unknown, he found her temporary home, only to learn that she, with her father Mons. De L'Ecluse (who was of course Walter), had just sailed for the New World. But the woman of the house gave him a slip of paper which the fair one had left for him in case he called and asked concerning her. On it was written this enigmatical lure : —

> I have drunk of the waters of Lethe,
> Hope yet remains to me.

Now, he would not have been an ideal court-lover, nor indeed but a sorry hero, if, after such a message, he had not promply sailed after the possible Christine. He learned that the vessel which bore her was to land at Biloxi, Louisiana. He sailed for the same port with his fortune in his pockets. But on arriving in Louisiana, Walter (or Mons. De L'Ecluse) had taken the disguising name of Walter Holden, and Christine posed as his daughter, Augustine Holden ; so her knight-errant thus lost trace of her. Christine-Augustine and her father settled in the Colonie Roland on the Red River. D'Aubant, with sixty colonists, founded a settlement but fifty miles away, which he named the Valley of Christine. Of course in due time the lovers met, and disguise was impossible and futile, and Augustine confessed her identity with the Crown Princess. As her husband Alexis had by this time conveniently died in prison, in Moscow, where he had been tried and condemned to death (and probably been privately executed), there was no reason, save the memory of her past exalted position, why she should not become the wife of an honest planter. They were married by a Spanish priest, and lived for twenty happy years in the Valley of Christine.

But D'Aubant's health failed, and he sought physicians in Paris. One day when Christine was walking in the garden of the Tuileries, with her two daughters, the children of D'Aubant, the German conversation of the mother attracted the attention of Marshal Saxe, who was the son of the very Countess Königsmark who had aided Chris-

tine's escape. The marshal recognized the
princess at once, in spite of the lapse of
years, and through his influence with Louis
XV. obtained for D'Aubant a commission as
major of troops, and the office of governor
of the Isle of Bourbon. The King also
informed the Empress of Austria, who was
a niece of Christine, that her aunt was alive;
and an invitation was sent from the Empress
for the D'Aubant family to become resi-
dents of the Austrian Court. They remained,
however, at the Isle of Bourbon until the
death of D'Aubant and the two daughters,
when Christine came to Brunswick and was
granted a pension for life by the Empress.
Her death in a convent, and her burial, took
place over half a century after her pretended legal demise.

This is the Christine of romance, of court
gossip, of court credulity, but there is another aspect of her story. Judge Martin
has written a standard history of Louisiana.
In it he says : —

Two hundred German settlers of Law's grant
were landed in the month of March 1721 at Biloxi out of the twelve hundred who had been
recruited. There came among the German new-

comers a female adventurer. She had been attached to the wardrobe of the wife of the Czaro-
witz Alexis Petrovitz, the only son of Peter the
Great. She imposed on the credulity of many
persons, particularly on that of an officer of the
garrison of Mobile (called by Bossu, the Chevalier D'Aubant, and by the King of Prussia, Wal-
deck), who, having seen the princess at St. Petersburg imagined he recognized her features in
those of her former servant, and gave credit to
the report that she was the Duke of Wolfenbut-
tels daughter, and the officer married her.

Grimm and Voltaire in their letters, Le-
vesque in his History, all unite in pronoun-
cing her an impostor. But you can choose
your own estimate of this creature of high
romance ; if you elect to deem her a princess, you find yourself in the goodly company of the King of France, the Empress of
Austria, Marshal Saxe, and a vast number
of other folk of rank and intelligence.

In the year 1771 there was sent to this
country from England a woman convict,
who had in her enforced home a most extraordinary and romantic career of successful fraud.

The first account which I have seen of

her was printed in the *Gentleman's Magazine* in 1771, and told simply of her startling intrusion into the Queen's apartments in London; but Dr. Doran's *Lives of the Queens of England of the House of Hanover* gives this account of this interesting bit of Anglo-American romance.

Sarah Wilson, yielding to a strong temptation in the year 1771, filched one or two of the Queen's jewels, and was condemned to be executed. It was considered almost a violation of justice that the thief should be saved from the halter and be transported instead of hanged. She was sent to America, where she was allotted as slave, or servant, to a Mr. Dwale, Bud Creek, Frederick County. Queen Charlotte would have thought nothing more of her, had her majesty not heard with some surprise, that her sister Susannah Caroline Matilda was keeping her court in the plantations. Never was surprise more genuine than the Queen's; it was exceeded only by her hilarity when it was discovered that the Princess Susannah was simply Sarah Wilson, at large. That somewhat clever girl having stolen a Queen's jewels, thought nothing, after escaping from the penal service to which she was condemned, of passing herself off as a Queen's sister. The Americans were not so acute as their descendants; so in love were some of them with the greatness they affected to despise, that they paid royal honors to the clever impostor. She passed the most joyous of seasons before she was consigned again to increase of penalty for daring to pretend relationship with the consort of King George. The story of the presuming girl, whose escapades, however, were not fully known in England at that time, served, as far as knowledge of them had reached the court, to amuse the gossips who had assembled about the cradle of the young Elizabeth.

In this account of Dr. Doran's there are some errors. The real story of the crime of Sarah Wilson and her subsequent career was this. In August, 1770, a strange woman found her way by means of a private staircase to the apartments of Queen Charlotte. She entered a room where the Queen and the Duchess of Ancaster were sitting, to their alarm. While she was taking a leisurely survey of the contents of the room, a page was summoned, who expelled the intruder, but did not succeed in arresting her. Shortly after, the Queen's apartments were broken into by a thief, who stole valuable jewels and a miniature of the Queen. The thief proved to be a woman named Sarah Wilson, who had been maid of the Honorable Miss Vernon, and this thief was asserted to be the inquisitive intruder whose visit had so alarmed the Queen.

Sarah Wilson was arrested, tried as a felon, and sentenced to death ; but by the exertions and influence of her former mistress the sentence was commuted to transportation to the American colonies for a seven years' term of servitude. This leniency caused considerable stir in London and some dissatisfaction.

In 1771, after passage in a convict ship, Sarah Wilson was sold to a Mr. William Duvall, of Bush Creek, Frederick County, Maryland, for seven years' servitude. After a short time, in which she apparently developed her plans of fraud, she escaped from her master, and went to Virginia and the Carolinas, where she assumed the title of Princess Susannah Caroline Matilda, and asserted she was the sister of the Queen of England. She still owned the miniature of the Queen, and some rich jewels, which gave apparent proof of her assertion, and it is said some rich clothing. It is indeed mysterious that a transported convict could retain in her possession, through all her reverses, the very jewels for whose theft she was punished; yet the story can scarcely be doubted.

She travelled through the South from plantation to plantation, with plentiful promises of future English offices and court favors to all who assisted her progress; and liberal sums of money were placed at her disposal, to be repaid by Queen Charlotte; and she seems to have been universally welcomed and feasted.

But the fame of the royal visitor spread afar and found its way to Bush Creek, to the ears of Mr. Duvall, and he promptly suspected that he had found trace of his ingenious runaway servant. As was the custom of the day, he advertised for her and a reward for her capture. The notice reads thus:—

Bush Creek, Frederick County, Maryland, October 11, 1771. Ran away from the subscriber a convict servant named SARAH WILSON, but has changed her name to Lady Susannah Caroline Matilda, which made the public believe that she was her Majesty's sister. She has a blemish in her right eye, black roll'd hair, stoops in the shoulders, and makes a common practice of writing and marking her clothes with a crown and a B. Whoever secures the said servant woman or will take her home, shall receive five pistoles, besides all cost of charges. William Duvall.

I entitle Michael Dalton to search the city of Philadelphia, and from there to Charleston, for the said woman.

Beauty readily inspires confidence, and dignity commands it. But a woman with such scant personal charms, with a blemish in her eye and stooping shoulders, must have been most persuasive in conversation to have surmounted such obstacles. It is said that she was most gracious, yet commanding.

To elude Michael Dalton's authorized search from Philadelphia to Charleston, Sarah Wilson fled from her scenes of success, but also of too familiar and extensive acquaintance, to New York. But New York proved still too near to Maryland, so she took passage for Newport. Here her fame preceded her, for in the *Newport Mercury* of November 29, 1773, is this notice : —

Last Tuesday arrived here from New York the lady who has passed through several of the southern colonies under the name and character of CAROLINE MATILDA, Marchioness de Wald-grave, etc., etc.

I do not know the steps that led to her capture and removal, but at the end of the year the Marchioness was back on William Duvall's plantation, and bound to serve a redoubled term of years. It seems to be probable that she also suffered more ignoble punishment, for Judge Martin says in his *History of Louisiana:* —

A female driven for her misconduct from the service of a maid of honor of Princess Matilda, sister of George III., was convicted at the Old Bailey and transported to Maryland. She effected her escape before the expiration of her time, and travelled through Virginia and both the Carolinas personating the Princess, and levying contributions on the credulity of the planters and merchants and even some of the kings officers. She was at last arrested in Charleston, prosecuted and whipped.

I often wonder what became of the Brummagem princess, with her jewels and her personal blemishes; and I often fancy that I find traces of her career, still masquerading, still imposing on simple folk. For instance,

Rev. Manasseh Cutler wrote, at his home in Ipswich Hamlet, Mass., on January 25, 1775:

A lady came to our house who had made a great noise in the country, and has been made the occasion of various conjectures. She calls herself Caroline Augusta Harriet, Duchess of Brownstonburges. Says she has resided in the Court of England for several years, that she eloped from the palace of St. James. She appears to be a person of an extraordinary education, and well acquainted with things at Court, but she is generally supposed to be an impostor.

Three days later he writes that he "conveyed the extraordinary visitor to town in a chaise." With this glimpse of Sarah — if Sarah she were — visiting in a little New England town in a sober Puritan family, and riding off to Boston in a chaise with the pious Puritan preacher, she vanishes from our ken, to be obscured in the smoke of battle and the din of war, and forced to learn that to American patriots it was no endearing trait to pose as an English princess.

CHAPTER VII.

THE UNIVERSAL FRIEND.

SIR THOMAS BROWNE says that "all heresies, how gross soever, have found a welcome with the people." Certainly they have with the people, and specially they have with the Rhode Island people. The eighty-two pestilent heresies so sadly deplored by the Puritan divines found a home in Rhode Island and the Providence Plantations. It was not strange, therefore, that from the heart of Narragansett should spring one of the most remarkable and successful religious woman-fanatics the world has ever known. Jemima Wilkinson was born in the town of Cumberland, R. I., in 1758. Though her father was a poor farmer, she came of no mean stock. She was a descendant of English kings — of King Edward I. — and later of Lieutenant Wilkinson, of Cromwell's army, and she was a second cousin of Governor Stephen Hopkins and Commodore Hopkins.

When she was eight years old her mother died, leaving her to the care of older sisters, whom she soon completely dominated. She was handsome, fond of ease and dress, vain, and eager for attention. She was romantic and impressionable, and when a new sect of religious zealots, called Separatists, appeared in her neighborhood — a sect who rejected church organization and insisted upon direct guidance from heaven — she became one of the most regular attendants at their meetings.

She soon betook herself to solitude and study of the Bible, and seemed in deep reflection, and at last kept wholly to her room, and then went to bed. She was at that time but eighteen years old, and it scarcely seems possible that she deliberately planned out her system of life-long deception which proved so successful; but soon she began to see visions, which she described to her sisters and visitors, and interpreted to them.

Finally she fell in a deep trance, which lasted thirty-six hours, during which she scarcely breathed. About the middle of the second day, when surrounded by anxious watchers (who proved valuable witnesses in her later career), she rose up majestically, called for clothing, dressed herself, and walked about fully restored and calm, though pale. But she announced that Jemima Wilkinson had died, and that her body was now inhabited by a spirit whose mission was to deliver the oracles of God to mankind, and who was to be known henceforth by the name of the Universal Friend. It ought to be noted here that this girl of eighteen not only maintained these absurd claims of resurrection of the body and reincarnation, at that time, in the face of the expostulation and arguments of her relatives and friends, but also with unshaken firmness, and before all hearers, till the day of her death at the age of sixty-one.

On the first Sunday after her trance, the Universal Friend preached in the open air near her home to a large and excited gathering of people ; and she electrified her audience by her eloquence, her brilliant imagination, her extraordinary familiarity with the Scriptures, and her facility and force of application and quotation from them. Her success in obtaining converts was most marked from the first, as was her success in obtaining temporal comforts and benefits from these converts. In this she resembled the English religious adventuress, Johanna Southcote. For six years she lived at the house of Judge William Potter, in South Kingstown, R. I. This handsome house was known as the Abbey. He enlarged it by building a splendid suite of rooms for his beloved spiritual leader, on whom he lavished his large fortune.

Her success as a miracle-worker was not so great. She announced that on a certain date she would walk upon the water, but when, in the face of a large multitude, she reached the water's edge, she denounced the lack of faith of her followers, and refused to gratify their curiosity by trying the experiment. Nor did she succeed in her attempt to raise from the dead one Mistress Susanna Potter, the daughter of Judge Potter, who died during Jemima's residence at the Abbey. She managed, however, to satisfy fully her followers by foretelling events, interpreting dreams, and penetrating secrets, which she

worded by ingeniously mystic and easily ap-
plicable terms.

Her meetings and her converts were not
confined to Rhode Island. In southern
Massachusetts and Connecticut many joined
her band. In New Milford, Conn., her converts erected a meeting-house. In 1782 she
started out upon a new mission. With a
small band of her disciples she went to
Philadelphia, where she was cordially received and entertained by the Quakers. In
Worcester, Pa., her reception was enthu-
siastic. Scarce a diary of those times but
contains some allusion to her or her career.
In the journal of Jacob Hiltzeheimer, of
Philadelphia, I read : —

Aug. 15, 1783. Returning from church, I observed people crowded about the Free Quakers
meeting-house, and was told they were waiting
to see the wonderful Jemima Wilkinson who had
preached. I remained till she came out to get
in her chair. She had on a white hat but no cap,
and a white linen garment that covered her to
her feet.

Aug. 20, 1783. Went to the new Quaker
meeting-house on Arch Street to hear Jemima

Wilkinson preach. She looks more like a man than a woman.

May 22, 1788. I rode out to Cunninghams Centre House to hear the famous Jemima Wilkinson preach, and in the room where formerly a billiard table stood I saw and heard her. She spoke much in the New England dialect. She appeared to be about twenty-five years of age, her hair was dressed like that of a man, and she wore a black gown after the fashion of church ministers.

The manuscript diary of the Reverend John Pitman, of Providence, R. I., says: "Saw that poor deluded creature Jemima Wilkerson and a number of her dull followers standing staring at the cross-roads."

In the days of reaction after the excitement of the Revolution, many aspirations for a better social state prompted settlements in outlying portions of the Central States. Communities were founded, Utopias were planned, and soon the united body of people known as the Friend's followers decided to seek in the depths of the wilderness a new home. It was a bold undertaking, but the band had a bold commander, and above all, they were absolute in their confidence in her.

In no way was that confidence shown so remarkably as in the fact that the settlement
was made for her but without her. The
three delegates sent to find a place suitable
for their purpose reported in favor of the
region at the foot of Seneca Lake in the
State of New York. In 1788 the settlement
was made on the west shore of the lake by
twenty-five persons, on the primitive high-
way of the region, about a mile south of
Dresden, and it was named Jerusalem.

For over two years a band of determined
believers labored in this wilderness to prepare a home for their leader, who was comfortably carrying on her triumphant and
flattering progress in the large cities. Surrounded by Indians, and menaced by wild
beasts, they cleared the forests, and planted
wheat, and lived on scant food. During the
first year one family for six weeks had only
boiled nettles and bohea tea for nourishment.
When the cornfields yielded the second summer, a small grist-mill was built with incredi-
ble labor. When the well-fed and not at all
over-worked Friend arrived, she found an
orderly, industrious community of two hundred and sixty persons, who had built for

her a home and a meeting-house, and she at once settled down in comparative comfort in the midst of her flock.

The house which was occupied by the Friend was a log-house of humble pretensions; to this two or three houses were added, then upper stories were placed over all, and framed in. It stood in a fine garden, and by its side was a long building used as a workshop for the women of the settlement, where spinning, weaving, and sewing were constantly carried on. Near by stood the sugar grove, a most lucrative possession of the society. From this home the Friend and her steadfast followers would ride in imposing cavalcade, two by two, to meeting at the early settlement. With their handsome, broad-brimmed hats, substantial clothes, and excellent horses, they made a most notable and impressive appearance. Her second house was more pretentious and comparatively luxurious; in it she lived till the time of her death.

Jemima Wilkinson's followers were of no poor or ordinary stock. Many brought to her community considerable wealth. Into the wilderness went with her from Kings-

town, R. I., Judge William Potter and his
daughters; a family of wealthy Hazards;
Captain James Parker (brother of Sir Peter
Parker); four Reynolds sisters from a family
of dignity; Elizabeth Luther and seven children; members of the Card, Hunt, Sherman,
and Briggs families. From New Milford,
Conn., emigrated a number of Stones and
Botsfords, and from New Bedford many members of the influential Hathaway and Lawrence families. From Stonington and New
London went a large number of Barneses
and Browns and Davises; from Philadelphia
the entire family of Malins and the Sup-
plees; from Worcester, Pa., came a most important recruit, Daniel Wagener, with his
sister, and Jonathan Davis, and other well-
to-do and influential persons.

The most important converts to belief in
her doctrines, and pioneers for her, were
doubtless Judge Potter and Captain Parker,
both men of large wealth and unstinted liberality to their leader. The former had been
treasurer of the State of Rhode Island; the
latter had been also a magistrate for twenty
years in the same State. They were the
largest contributors to the fund for the pur-

chase of the tract of land in New York. These men sacrificed home and friends to come to the New Jerusalem with their adored priestess; but they quickly escaped from her sway, and became in later years her most powerful enemies. They even issued a complaint against her for blasphemy. The officer who tried to serve the warrant upon her was unable to seize the Friend, who was an accomplished rider and well mounted, and, when he went to her house, was roughly treated and driven away. John Lawrence, whose wife was Anna Hathaway, was a near relative of Commodore Lawrence; he was a shipbuilder at New Bedford, and, though he followed Jemima Wilkinson to Seneca Lake, never joined her society. Many of her believers never lived in her settlement, but visited her there; and many bequeathed to her liberally by will, and made valuable gifts to her during their life.

In the main, the influence of this remarkable woman continued unabated with a large number of her followers throughout her life, and even after her death. This power survived against the adverse conditions of frequent litigations, personal asperities, constant injurious reports, and the dislike of many to the strictness of her faith and austerity of life required by her from her followers. This allegiance could hardly have been founded solely on religious credulity, but must have depended largely in her attractive personal traits, her humanity, and doubtless also to her attractive expositions of her lively imagination. To the last she persisted in calling herself by the sole name of the Universal Friend. Even her will was signed thus : "I, the person once called Jemima Wilkinson, but in and ever since the year 1777 known as and called the Public Universal Friend, hereunto set my name and seal ; Public Universal Friend." But she cannily appended a sub-signature over a cross-mark of the name of her youth.

A remarkable feature of the Universal Friend's Society, perhaps the most remarkable effect of her teachings, was the large number of excellent women who, as persistent celibates, adhered to her teachings throughout their lives. Some lived in her house, and all were consistent representatives of her doctrines, and many lived to great old age. Nor can I doubt from the accounts of their lives that they were exceedingly happy in their celibacy and in their unwavering belief in Jemima Wilkinson. Carlyle says, "Man's gullibility is not his worst blessing." I may paraphrase his assertion thus — woman's gullibility is one of her most comforting traits. Her persistent belief, her unswerving devotion, often to wholly unworthy objects, brings its own reward in a lasting, though unreasoning satisfaction.

Jemima's male adherents were nearly all married. It was her intention that her property, which was considerable, should be held for the benefit of her followers who survived her, but it was gradually transferred and wasted till the last aged members of the band were forced to depend upon the charity of neighbors and the public.

One of the best accounts of the personality of Jemima Wilkinson was given by the Duke de la Rochefoucault Liancourt, who visited her in 1796. He says : —

We saw Jemima and attended her meeting, which is held in her own house. Jemima stood at the door of her bed chamber on a carpet, with an armchair behind her. She had on a white

morning gown and a waistcoat such as men wear
and a petticoat of the same color. Her black
hair was cut short, carefully combed and divided
behind into three ringlets; she wore a stock and
a white silk cravat, which was tied about her neck
with affected negligence. In point of delivery
she preached with more ease than any other
Quaker I have ever heard, but the subject matter
of her discourse was an eternal repetition of the
same subjects — death, sin and repentance. She
is said to be about forty years of age but did
not appear more than thirty. She is of middle
stature, well made, of florid countenance, and
has fine teeth and beautiful eyes. Her action is
studied. She aims at simplicity but is pedantic
in her manner. Her hypocrisy may be traced in
all her discourse, actions and conduct and even
in the very manner which she manages her countenance.

He speaks with much asperity of her pretence of condemning earthly enjoyment while
her whole manner of living showed much personal luxury and gratification.

This description of her was given by one
who saw her : —

She was higher than a middle stature, of fine
form, fair complexion with florid cheeks, dark
and brilliant eyes, and beautiful white teeth.

Her hair dark auburn or black, combed from the seam of the head and fell on her shoulders in three full ringlets. In her public addresses she would rise up and stand perfectly still for a minute or more, than proceed with a slow and distinct enunciation. She spoke with great ease and increased fluency; her voice clear and harmonious, and manner persuasive and emphatic. Her dress rich but plain and in a style entirely her own; a broad brimmed beaver hat with a low crown, and the sides when she rode turned down and tied under her chin; a full light drab cloak or mantle and a unique underdress; and a cravat round the neck with square ends that fell down to the waist forward.

The square cravat or band gave her a semi-clerical look. The rich glossy smoothness and simplicity of dressing her hair is commented on by nearly all who left accounts of her personal appearance; and was doubtless more marked in her day because the feminine headdress of that time was elaborate to a degree that was even fantastic, and was at the opposite extreme from simple curls.

Many scurrilous and absurd stories are told of her, especially in a biography of her which was written and printed soon after her death. Many of the anecdotes in this biography are too petty and too improbable to be given any credence. I am convinced that she was a woman of most sober and discreet life; importunate of respect and greedy of absolute power; personally luxurious in her tastes, and of vast ambition, but always of dignified carriage. And through her dignity, sobriety, and reserve she had a lasting hold upon her followers. Perhaps she told her alleged belief, her tale of her mission, until she half believed it herself. One story of her is worthy repetition, and I think of credence.

It tells of her repulse when she endeavored to secure among her followers the Indians of Canandaigua. She spoke to them at Canandaigua and again at Seneca Lake, evidently realizing fully the advantage that might be gained from them through land-grants and personal support. Many of the Oneida Indians had been converted by missionaries to Christianity, and as they held a Sunday service she entered and made a thrilling and impressive address, assuring them she was their Saviour Jesus Christ. They listened to her with marked attention, and one of their number arose and delivered a short and animated speech to his companions in the Oneida tongue. When he ceased speaking, Jemima turned to the interpreter and asked an explanation of the speaker's words, which was given her. The Indian speaker sat by her side with a sardonic expression on his grim face, and when the interpretation was finished, said significantly and coldly, "You no Jesus Christ — he know all poor Indian say as well as what white man say," and turned contemptuously from her. It is said that the cunning Indian detective was the great chief Red Jacket, and from what we know of his shrewd and diplomatic character it can readily be believed.

CHAPTER VIII.

EIGHTEENTH–CENTURY MANNERS.

NOTHING can more plainly show the regard in which women were held in Virginia in the middle of the eighteenth century than the entries in the accounts of Colonel William Byrd of his visits to Virginia homes. He was an accomplished and cultivated gentleman, who wrote with much intelligence and power when relating his interviews with men, or discussing what might be termed masculine subjects, but who revealed his opinion of the mental capacity of the fair sex by such side glimpses as these: "We supped about nine and then prattled with the ladies." "Our conversation with the ladies was like whip-syllabub, very pretty but nothing in it." He also makes rather coarse jokes about Miss Thekky and her maiden state, which was of course most deplorable in his and every one else's eyes; and he alludes disparagingly to Mrs.

Chiswell as "one of those absolute rarities, a very good old woman." The Virginia women are said by other authors of that day to have been "bounteous in size and manner." M. Droz wrote of them : —

Most of the women are quite pretty and insinuating in their manner if they find you so. When you ask them if they would like to have husbands they reply with a good grace that it is just what they desire.

For many years an epidemic of sentimentality and mawkishness seemed to everywhere prevail in America, and indeed everywhere among English-speaking peoples, and seemed also to be universally admired. The women in America were, as Doctor Shippen wrote, "languishingly sweet." This insipidity pervaded the letters of the times, it showed in all the diaries and journals that record conversations. Long and vapid discourses on love and matrimony and "Platonicks" were held even between comparative strangers. Even so sprightly and intelligent a journalist as Sally Wister records her exceedingly flippant conversation with young officers of new acquaintance, who, within a few hours of introduction, suggested matrimony and love and kisses, and punctuated their remarks with profanity, which they "declared was their favorite vice."

William Black, a most observant traveller, wrote of Philadelphia girls in 1744 : —

One of the ladies began a discourse on love wherein she pull'd the other Sex to pieces. Setting forth the Constancy of their Sex and the Unstability of ours. Every one of the young ladies put in an Oar and helped her Out ; at last being quite tired of the Subject and at a Loss what more to say the Lady that begun it turned from it artfull enough to Criticizing on Plays and their Authors, Addison, Otway, Prior, Congreve, Dryden, Pope, Shakespere &c were named often in Question ; the words Genius and no Genius, Invention, Poetry, Fine things, bad Language, no Style, Charming writing, Imagary and Diction, with many more Expressions which swim on the surface of Criticism seemed to have been caught by the Female Fishers for the Reputation of Wit.

Though William Black was willing to talk of "Love and Platonicks," and with warm approval, he was bitter in his rebuke of this "Fine Lady Mrs Talkative" who dared to speak of books and authors.

It is well to note the books read by these young ladies in high life, and their critical opinion of them. A much-liked book was named *The Generous Inconstant.* It has vanished from our modern view. I should really like to see the book that rejoiced in such a title. We can also learn of the books read by Lucinda the "Young lady of Virginia" and her friend Polly Brent. Lucinda's journal was written during a visit to the Lees, Washingtons, Grymes, Spotswoods, and other first families of Virginia, and has been preserved till our own day. She thus records : —

I have spent the morning in reading Lady Julia Mandeville, and was much affected. Indeed I think I never cried more in my life reading a Novel; the Stile is beautiful, but the tale is horrid. Some one just comes to tell us Mr Masenbird and Mr Spotswood is come. We must go down, but I am affraid both Sister's and my eyes will betray us.

Mrs. A. Washington has lent me a new Novel called Victoria. I cant say I admire the Tale, though I think it prettyly Told. There is a Verse in it I wish you much to read. I believe if I ant too Lazy I will copy it off for you; the verse is not very beautifull but the sense is I assure you.

I have been very agreeably entertained this evening reading a Novel called Malvern Dale. It is something like Evelina, though not so pretty. I have a piece of advice to give which I have before urged, that is to read something improving. Books of instruction will be a thousand times more pleasing (after a little while) than all the novels in the World. I own myself I am too fond of Novel-reading; but by accustoming myself to reading other Books I have become less so. I have entertained myself all day reading Telemachus. It is really delightful and very improving.

I have for the first time in my life just read Pope's Eloiza. I had heard my Polly extol it frequently, and curiosity led me to read it. I will give you my opinion of it; the Poetry I think butifull, but do not like some of the sentiments. Some of Eloizas is too Amorous for a Female I think.

Sally Wister, a girl of fifteen, had brought to her what she called "a charming collection of books," — *Caroline Melmoth,* some *Lady's Magazines, Juliet Grenville* and "Joe Andrews" — this, Fielding's *Joseph Andrews,* I suppose.

The sensible and intelligent Eliza Lucas wrote in 1742, when she was about twenty-one years old, with much critical discrimination on what she read : —

I send by the bearer the last volume of Pamela. She is a good girl and as such I love her dearly, but I must think her very defective, and even blush for her while she allows herself that disgusting liberty of praising herself, or what is very like it, repeating all the fine speeches made to her by others, — when a person distinguished for modesty in every other respect should have chosen rather to conceal them, or at least let them come from some other hand ; especially as she might have considered those high compliments might have proceeded from the partiality of her friends, or with a view to encourage her and make her aspire after those qualifications which are ascribed to her, which I know experimentally to be often the case.   But then you answer, she was a young country girl, had seen nothing of life, and it was natural for her to be pleased with praise, and she had not art enough to conceal it.   True, before she was Mrs. B. it was excusable when only wrote to her father and mother, but after she had the advantage of Mr B's conversation, and others of sense and distinction, I must be of another opinion.   But here arises a difficulty — we are to be made acquainted by the author of all particulars ; how then is it to be done ? I think by Miss Durnford or some other lady very intimate with Mrs B. How you smile at my presumption for instructing one so far above my own level as the author of Pamela (whom I esteem much for the regard he pays to virtue and religion) but contract your smile into a mortified look for I acquit the author. He designed to paint no more than a woman, and he certainly designed it as a reflection upon the vanity of our sex that a character so complete in every other instance should be so defective in this. Defective indeed when she sometimes mentions that poor creature Mr H's applauses it puts me in mind of the observation in Don Quixote, how grateful is praise even from a madman.

A most popular form of literary intercourse and amusement was everywhere found in stilted sentimental correspondence, conducted often under assumed and high-sounding names, usually classical. For instance, this young lady of Virginia writes to her friend, plain Polly, when separated for a short time : —

Oh my Marcia how hard is our fate ! that we should be deprived of your dear company, when it would compleat our Felecity — but such is the fate of Mortals! We are never permitted to be perfectly happy. I suppose it is all right, else the Supreme Disposer of all things would have not permitted it, we should perhaps have been more neglectful than we are of our duty.

She frequently forgets to use the pompous name of Marcia, especially when writing on any subject that really interests her : —

You may depend upon it Polly this said Matrimony alters us mightily. I am afraid it alienates us from every one else. It is I fear the ban of Female Friendship. Let it not be with ours Polly if we should ever Marry. Farewell my love, may Heaven shower blessings on your head prays your Lucinda. (I always forget to make use of our other name.)

Even so sensible and intelligent a woman as Abigail Adams corresponded under the names Diana or Portia, while her friends masqueraded as Calliope, Myra, Aspasia, and Aurelia. Wives wrote to their husbands, giving them fanciful or classical names. This of course was no new fashion. Did not Shakespeare write : —

> Adoptedly — as school-maids change their name
> By vain though apt affection.

It is evident that in spite of all the outward dignity shown in these pompous forms of address, and in a most ceremonial and reserved bearing in public, there existed in private life much rudeness of demeanor and much freedom in manner. Let me quote again from the vivacious pages of the young lady of Virginia : —

The Gentlemen dined today at Mr Massinbirds. We have supped, and the gentlemen are not returned yet. Lucy and myself are in a peck of troubles for fear they should return drunk. Sister has had our bed moved in her room. Just as we were undress'd and going to bed the Gentlemen arrived, and we had to scamper. Both tipsy!

Today is Sunday. Brother was so worsted by the frolick yesterday, we did not set off today. Mr C. Washington returned today from Fredericksburg. You cant think how rejoiced Hannah was, nor how dejected in his absence she always is. You may depend upon it Polly this said Matrimony alters us mightely. Hannah and myself were going to take a long walk this evening but were prevented by the two Horred Mortals Mr Pinkard and Mr Washington, who siezed and kissed me a dozen times in spite of all the resistance I could make. They really think, now

they are married, they are prevaliged to do anything. . . .

When we got here we found the house pretty
full. I had to dress in a great hurry for dinner.
We spent the evening very agreeably in chatting.
Milly Washington is a thousand times prettyer
than I thought her at first and very agreeable.
About sunset Nancy, Milly and myself took a
walk in the Garden (it is a most beautiful place).
We were mighty busy cutting thistles to try our
sweethearts, when Mr Washington caught us;
and you cant conceive how he plagued us —
chased us all over the Garden and was quite
impertinent. I must tell you of our frolic after
we went to our room. We took a large dish of
bacon and beef; after that, a bowl of Sago
cream; and after that an apple-pye. While we
were eating the apple-pye in bed — God bless
you, making a great noise — in came Mr Washington dressed in Hannah's short gown and peti-
coat, and seazed me and kissed me twenty times,
in spite of all the resistance I could make; and
then Cousin Molly. Hannah soon followed
dressed in his Coat. They joined us in eating
the apple-pye and then went out. After this we
took it into our heads to want to eat oysters. We
got up, put on our rappers and went down in the
Seller to get them; do you think Mr Washington
did not follow us and scear us just to death. We

went up tho, and eat our oysters. We slept in the old ladys room too, and she sat laughing fit to kill herself at us.

Now, these were no folk of low degree. The lively and osculatory Mr. Washington was Corbin Washington. He married Hannah, daughter of Richard Henry Lee. Their grandson, John A. Washington, was the last of the family to occupy Mount Vernon. Mr. Pinkard also had a delicate habit of " bolting in upon us, and overhearing part of our conveasation in our rooms, which hily delighted him," trying to seize the girls' letters, dressing in women's clothes, and other manly and gentlemanly pleasantries.

Sarah Eve records in her journal an equally affectionate state of manners in Philadelphian society in 1722. She writes : —

In the morning Dr Shippen came to see us. What a pity it is that the Doctor is so fond of kissing. He really would be much more agreeable if he were less fond. One hates to be always kissed, especially as it is attended with so many inconveniences. It decomposes the economy of ones handkerchief, it disorders ones high roll, and it ruffles the serenity of ones countenance.

Though there was great talk made of gallant and chivalric bearing toward the ladies, it is evident that occasional rudeness of manner still existed. A writer in the *Royal Gazette* of August 16, 1780, thus complains of New York swains : —

As the Mall seems to be the chief resort for company of an evening I am surprized that there is no more politeness and decorum observ'd by the masculine gender. In short there is seldom a seat in that agreeable walk that is not taken up by the gentlemen. This must be very disagreeable to the fair sex in general whose tender delicate limbs may be tired with the fatigues of walking, and bend, denied a seat to rest them.

I cannot discover that anything of the nature of our modern chaperonage was known in colonial days. We find the early travellers such as Dunton taking many a long ride with a fair maid a-pillion back behind them. In 1750 Captain Francis Goelet made a trip through New England. He consorted only with the fashionable folk of the day, and he appeared to find in them a very genial and even countrified simplicity of manners. He tells of riding to "Turtle

Frolicks" and country dances with young ladies of refinement and good station in life. To one of the finer routs at Cambridge he rode with Miss Betty Wendell in a chaise. There were twenty couples in all who went to this Frolick, all, he says complacently, the "Best Fashion in Boston." Young men escorted young girls to dancing-parties, and also accompanied them home after the dance was finished.

Weddings were everywhere, throughout the middle and southern colonies, scenes of great festivity.

I have been much interested and amused in reading the *Diary of Jacob Hiltzheimer*, of Philadelphia (which has recently been published), to note his references to the deep drinking at the weddings of the day. One entry, on February 14, 1767, runs thus : " At noon went to William Jones to drink punch, met several of my friends and got decently drunk. The groom could not be accused of the same fault." This cheerful frankness reminds us of Sir Walter Raleigh's similar ingenuous expression : " Some of our captains garoused of wine till they were reasonable pleasant."

This William Jones was married eighteen years later to a third wife, and again kept open house, and once more friend Jacob called on the bride and ate the wedding-cake and drank the wedding-punch. Nay, more, he called four days in succession, and at the end " rode all the afternoon to wear off the effects of the punch and clear my head." At one bride's house, Mrs. Robert Erwin's, record was kept that for two days after the wedding, between three and four hundred gentlemen had called, drank punch, and probably kissed the bride.

It was the universal Philadelphia custom for the groom's friends to call thus for two days at his house and drink punch, and every evening for a week large tea-parties were given by the bride, the bridesmaids and groomsmen always in attendance. Sometimes a coaching trip was taken by the entire bridal party out on the Lancaster pike, for a wedding breakfast.

Similar customs prevailed in New York. In a letter written by Hannah Thompson I read of bridal festivities in that town.

The Gentlemans Parents keep Open house just in the same manner as the Brides Parents.

The Gentlemen go from the Bridegroom house to drink punch with and give Joy to his Father. The Brides visitors go in the same manner from the Brides to her mothers to pay their compliments to her. There is so much driving about at these times that in our narrow streets there is some danger. The Wedding house resembles a beehive. Company perpetually flying in and out.

In a new country, with novel methods of living, and unusual social relations, there were some wild and furious wooings. None were more coarsely extraordinary than the courting of young Mistress Burwell by the Governor of the colony of Virginia, an intemperate, blustering English ruffian named Nicholson. He demanded her hand in an Orientally autocratic manner, and when neither she nor her parents regarded him with favor, his rage and determination knew no bounds. He threatened the lives of her father and mother "with mad furious distracted speech." When Parson Fouace came, meekly riding to visit poor Mr. Burwell, his parishioner, who was sick (naturally enough), the Governor set upon him with words of abuse, pulled the clerical hat off, drew his sword, and threatened the clerical life, until the parson fled in dismay. Fancying that the brother of Commissary Blair, the President of the Virginia College, was a would-be suitor to his desired fair one, he assailed the President with insane jealousy, saying, " Sir, your brother is a villain and you have betrayed me," and he swore revenge on the entire family. To annoy further the good President, he lent his pistols to the wicked college boys that they might thus keep the President out of the 'college buildings. He vowed if Mistress Burwell married any one but himself he would cut the throat of bridegroom, minister, and justice who issued the marriage license. The noise of his abuse reached England, and friends wrote from thence protesting letters to him. At last the Council united and succeeded in procuring his removal. Poor President Blair did not fare well under other governors, and both College and President were fiercely hated by Governor Andros ; and "a sparkish young gentleman," the grandfather of Martha Washington's first husband, to show his zeal for his gubernatorial friend, went into church and " with great fury and violence "

pulled Mrs. Blair out of her pew in the face
of the minister and the whole congregation
— and this in the stately old cavalier days.

One very curious duty devolved on young
girls at that day. They often served as
pall-bearers. At the funeral of Mrs. Daniel
Phœnix the pall-bearers were women, and
when Mrs. John Morgan, sister of Francis
Hopkinson, died in Philadelphia, her brother
wrote of her funeral : —

The morning was snowy and severely cold,
and the walking very dangerous and slippery,
never the less a number of respectable citizens
attended the funeral and the pall was borne by
the first ladies of the place.

Sarah Eve, in her diary, writes in 1772, in
a somewhat flippant manner : " R. Rush, P.
Dunn, K. Vaughan, and myself carried Mr.
Ash's child to be buried ; foolish custom for
girls to prance it through the streets without
hats or bonnets!" At the funeral of Fanny
Durdin in 1812, the girl pall-bearers
were dressed in white, and
wore long white
veils.

CHAPTER IX.

THEIR AMUSEMENTS AND ACCOMPLISHMENTS.

OF amusements for women in the first century of colonial life, we can almost say there were none. There was in New England no card-playing, no theatre-going, no dancing. The solemn Thursday lecture was the sole mid-week gathering. Occasionally there was the excitement of Training Day. In the South the distances were too great from plantation to plantation for frequent friendly meetings. As time went on, coöperation in gathering and storing the various food-harvests afforded opportunities for social intercourse. Apple-parings and corn-huskings were autumnal delights, but when these were over, the chafing youth found no recreations through the long, snowy months in country homes, and but scant opportunity for amusement in town. No wonder that they turned eagerly to the singing-school, and found in that innocent gathering

a safety-valve for the pent-up longing for
diversion which burned in young souls then
as now. We can but wonder how, ere the
singing-school became a force, young New
Englanders became acquainted enough with
each other to think of marriage; and we
can almost regard the establishment of the
study of fugue and psalm singing as the
preservation of the commonwealth.

In Virginia the different elements of life
developed characteristic pastimes, and by the
first quarter of the eighteenth century there
were opportunities of diversion offered for
women.

We have preserved to us an exact account of the sports which were enjoyed by
both Virginian men and women. It may be
found in the *Virginia Gazette* for October,
1737 : —

We have advices from Hanover County that
on St Andrews Day there are to be Horse Races
and several other Diversions for the entertainment of the Gentlemen and Ladies, at the Old
Field, near Captain John Bickertons, in that
County if permitted by the Hon Wm Byrd Esq
Proprietor of said land, the substance of which
is as follows viz :

It is proposed that 20 Horses or Mares do run around a three mile course for a prize of five pounds.

That a Hat of the value of 20s be cudgelled for, and that after the first challenge made the Drums are to beat every Quarter of an hour for three challenges round the Ring and none to play with their Left hand.

That a violin be played for by 20 Fiddlers; no person to have the liberty of playing unless he bring a fiddle with him. After the prize is won they are all to play together and each a different tune, and to be treated by the company.

That 12 Boys of 12 years of age do run 112 yards for a hat of the cost of 12 shillings.

That a Flag be flying on said Day 30 feet high.

That a handsome entertainment be provided for the subscribers and their wives; and such of them as are not so happy as to have wives may treat any other lady.

That Drums Trumpets Hautboys &c be provided to play at said entertainment.

That after Dinner the Royal Health His Honor the Governor's &c are to be drunk.

That a Quire of Ballads be sung for by a number of Songsters, all of them to have liquor sufficient to clear their Wind Pipes.

That a pair of Silver Buckles be wrestled for by a number of brisk young men.

That a pair of handsome Shoes be danced for.

That a pair of handsome Silk Stockings of one Pistole value be given to the handsomest young country maid that appears in the field.

With many other whimsical and Comical Diversions too numerous to mention.

And as this mirth is designed to be purely innocent and void of offence, all persons resorting there are desired to behave themselves with decency and sobriety; the subscribers being resolved to discountenance all immorality with the utmost rigor.

There is a certain rough and noisy heartiness in this rollicking Racing Day in old Virginia that speaks of boisterous cheer akin to the days of "merrie England," and which seems far from disagreeable when contrasted with the dull yearly round of sober days in New England. Virginia and Maryland men had many social clubs "to promote innocent mirth and ingenious humour," but of course within these clubs their consorts and daughters were not guests. A ball or a country dance were the chief amusements of Southern women, and very smart functions some of these balls were, though they did begin in broad daylight.

An early account was given by a travelling Virginian, William Black, of a Government Ball in the Council Room at Annapolis in 1744.

The Ladies of Note made a Splendant Appearance. In a Room Back from where they Danc'd was Several Sorts of Wines, Punch and Sweetmeats. In this Room those that was not engaged in any Dancing Match might better employ themselves at Cards, Dice, Backgammon, or with a cheerful Glass. The Ladies were so very agreeable and seem'd so intent on Dancing that one might have Imagin'd they had some Design on the Virginians, either Designing to make Tryal of their Strength and Vigour, or to convince them of their Activity and Sprightliness. After several smart engagements in which no advantage on either side was Observable, with a mutual Consent about 1 of the Clock in the Morning it was agreed to break up, every Gentleman waiting on his Partner home.

The method in which a ball was conducted somewhat more than a century ago in Louisville was thus told by Maj. Samuel S. Forman, who visited that town as a young man.

After the managers had organized the Company by drawing numbers and appointing the opening with a Minuet, Uncle was called on and introduc'd to a Lady for the opening scene. The Managers who distributed the numbers called Gent[n] No. 1, he takes his stand — Lady No. 1, she rises from her seat, the Manager leads her to the floor and introduces Gent[n] No. 1, & so on till the floor is full. After all the Company have been thus call'd out then the Gent[n] are free to seek his Partner but no monopoly. Lady at the head chooses the figure, but it is considered out of order for one Lady to head a figure twice unless all have been at the head. If there happen to be some ladies to whom from mistake or otherwise have been passed the Managers duty is to see to it. And another Custom was for a Gent[n] to call on a Lady & inform her of an intended ball & ask permission to see her to the place & see her safe home again. If the Gent[n] does not draw such Lady for the first Contra Dance he generally engages her for the first Volunteer. At the Refreshments the Gent[n] will by instinct without Chesterfieldian monition see that his betterhalf (for the time being) has a *quantum sufficit* and that without cramming his jaws full until he has reconducted her to the ball-room, then he is at liberty to absent himself for a while. There were two young gentlemen there from

New York who were much attached to each other. They promised to let each other know when a ball was on foot. At one time one came to the other and told him to prepare his pumps against such an evening. The answer was — Pumps out of order, must decline. No Sir that will not do. Then Sir you have been buying Several pair of handsome Mocassons for New York Ladies. If you will lend me one pair & you will put on one pair (it wont hurt them) I will go. Snaps his fingers — the very thing. The next ball after this Moccasons became very fashionable. So many fashions have their origins from Necessity.

A traveller named Bennet gives us an account of the amusements of Boston women in the middle of the century, when dancing was slowly becoming fashionable.

For their domestic amusements every afternoon after drinking tea, the gentlemen and ladies walk the Mall, and from there adjourn to one anothers house to spend the evening, those that are not disposed to attend the evening lecture which they may do if they please six nights in the seven the year round. What they call the Mall is a walk on a fine green Common adjoining to the south east side of the town. The Government being in the hands of dissenters they dont admit of plays or music houses; but of late they have sent up an assembly to which some of the ladies resort. But they are looked upon to be none of the nicest, in regard to their reputation, and it is thought it will be soon suppressed for it is much taken notice of and exploded by the religious and sober part of the people. But notwithstanding plays and such like diversions do not obtain here, they dont be dispirited or moped for the want of them; for both the ladies and gentlemen dress and appear as gay in common as courtiers in England on a coronation or birthday. And the ladies visit here, drink tea, indulge in every little piece of gentility to the height of the mode, and neglect the affairs of the family with as good a grace as the finest ladies in London.

The Marquis de Chastellux writes of the Philadelphia assembly in 1780 : —

The assembly or subscription ball, of which I must give an account may here be introduced. At Philadelphia, there are places appropriated for the young people to dance in and where those whom that amusement does not suit may play at different games of cards, but at Philadelphia games of commerce are alone allowed. A manager or Master of Ceremonies presides at

the methodical amusements ; he presents to the
gentlemen and lady dancers, billets folded up
containing each a number ; thus fate decides the
male or female partner for the whole evening.
All the dances are previously arranged and the
dancers are called in their turns. These dances,
like the toasts we drink at table, have some re-
lation to politics ; one is called The Successful
Campaign, another Bourgoynes Defeat, a third
Clintons Retreat. The managers are generally
chosen from among the most distinguished officers of the army. Colonel Mitchell, a little fat
squat man, was formerly the manager, but when
I saw him he had descended from the magistracy
and danced like a common citizen. He is said
to have exercised his office with great severity,
and it is told of him, that a young lady who was
figuring in a country dance, having forgot her
turn through conversing with a friend, he came
up to her and called out aloud, " Give over, Miss,
take care what you are about. Do you think
you come here for your pleasure ? "

The dance, *A Successful Campaign*, was
the one selected by diplomatic Miss Peggy
Champlin to open the ball, when she danced
in Newport with General Washington, to the
piping of De Rochambeau and his fellow
officers. This was " the figure " of *A Suc-*

cessful Campaign. " Lead down two couples on the outside and up the middle ; second couple do the same, turn contrary partners, cast off, right hand and left." It was simple, was it not — but I doubt not it was dignified and of sedate importance when Washington footed it.

Stony Point was another favorite of Revolutionary days — for did not General Wayne successfully storm the place? This dance was more difficult ; the directions were somewhat bewildering. " First couple three hands round with the second lady — allemand. Three hands round with the second gentleman — allemand again. Lead down two couples, up again, cast off one couple, hands round with the third, right and left." I scarcely know what the figure "allemand" was. The German allemande was then an old style of waltz, slower than the modern waltz, but I can scarcely think that Washington or any of those serious, dignified officers waltzed, even to slow time.

Another obsolete term is "foot it."

> Come and foot it as you go
> On the light fantastic toe,

seems to refer to some definite step in dancing. Sheridan in *The Rivals* thus uses the term in regard to dances : —

I 'd foot it with e'er a captain in the county, but these outlandish heathen allemandes and cotillions are quite beyond me.

But "footing it" and "outlandish heathen allemandes" are not so misty as another term, "to haze." In the *Innocent Maid* they "hazed." "First three couples haze, then lead down the middle and back again, close with the right hand and left." In dancing the *Corsino* they figured thus : "Three couples foot it and change sides; foot it again and once more change sides; three couples allemand, and the first fall in the middle then right hand and left."

Dancing-masters' advertisements of those days often give us the list of modish dances : "Allemandes Vally's, De la Cours, Devonshire Minuets and Jiggs."

Burnaby in 1759 wrote of a special pleasure of the Quaker maids of Philadelphia : of fishing-parties.

The women are exceedingly handsome and polite. They are naturally sprightly and fond of

pleasure and upon the whole are much more
agreeable and accomplished than the men. Since
their intercourse with the English officers they
are greatly improved, and without flattery, many
of them would not make bad figures even in the
first assemblies in Europe. Their amusements
are chiefly dancing in the winter, and in the
summer forming parties of pleasure upon the
Schuilkill, and in the country. There is a society of sixteen ladies and as many gentlemen
called The fishing company, who meet once a
fortnight upon the Schuilkill. They have a very
pleasant room erected in a romantic situation
upon the banks of that river where they generally dine and drink tea. There are several
pretty walks about it, and some wild and rugged
rocks which together with the water and fine
groves that adorn the banks, form a most beautiful and picturesque scene. There are boats and
fishing tackle of all sorts, and the company
divert themselves with walking, fishing, going up
the water, dancing, singing, conversing, or just
as they please. The ladies wear an uniform and
appear with great ease and advantage from the
neatness and simplicity of it. The first and
most distinguished people of the colony are of
this society ; and it is very advantageous to a
stranger to be introduced to it, as he hereby gets
acquainted with the best and most respectable

company in Philadelphia. In the winter when there is snow upon the ground it is usual to make what they call sleighing parties.

He says of New York society : —

The women are handsome and agreeable though rather more reserved than the Philadelphian ladies. Their amusements are much the same as in Pensylvania ; viz balls and sleighing expeditions in the winter, and in the summer going in parties upon the water and fishing ; or making excursions into the country. There are several houses pleasantly situated upon East River near New York where it is common to have turtle feasts ; these happen once or twice in a week. Thirty or forty gentlemen and ladies meet and dine together, drink tea in the afternoon, fish and amuse themselves till evening and then return home in Italian chaises, a gentleman and lady in each chaise. In the way there is a bridge, about three miles distant from New York which you always pass over as you return, called the Kissing Bridge where it is a part of the etiquette to salute the lady who has put herself under your protection.

It is evident from these quotations and from the testimony of other contemporary authors that one of the chief winter amuse-

ments in New York and Philadelphia and
neighboring towns was through sleighing-
parties. Madam Knights, of Boston, writing
in 1704 of her visit to New York, said : —

Their diversion in winter is riding sleighs
about three or four miles out of town where they
have houses of entertainment at a place called
the Bowery, and some go to friends houses, who
handsomely treat them. Mr. Burroughs carried
his spouse and daughter and myself out to one
Madam Dowes a gentlewoman that lived at a
farmhouse who gave us a handsome entertainment of five or six dishes and choice beer and
metheglin, etc, all which she said was the produce of her farm. I believe we met fifty or sixty
sleighs that day ; they fly with great swiftness
and some are so furious that they will turn out
of the path for none except a loaded cart.

There were few sleighs at that date in Boston.

Sixty-four years later, in 1768, a young
English officer, Alexander Macraby, wrote
thus to his brother of the pleasures of sleighing : —

You can never have had a party in a sleigh or
sledge I had a very clever one a few days ago.

Seven sleighs with two ladies and two men in each proceeded by fiddlers on horseback set out together upon a snow of about a foot deep on the roads to a public house, a few miles from town where we danced, sung, romped and eat and drank and kicked away care from morning till night, and finished our frolic in two or three side-boxes at the play. You can have no idea of the state of the pulse seated with pretty women mid-deep in straw, your body armed with furs and flannels, clear air, bright sunshine, spotless sky, horses galloping, every feeling turned to joy and jollity.

That older members of society then, as now, did not find sleighing parties altogether alluring, we learn from this sentence in a letter of Hannah Thompson written to John Mifflin in 1786 : —

This Slaying match Mr Houston of Houston St gave his Daughters, Dear Papa, Dear Papa, do give us a slaying — he at last consented, told them to get ready and dress themselves warm, which they accordingly did and came running. We are ready papa. He ordered the Servants to have some burnt wine against they came back. He desir'd them to step upstairs with him before they went. As soon as they got in an Attick chamber, he threw up all the windows and seated them in two old Arm Chairs and began to whip and Chirrup with all the Spirit of a Slaying party. And after he kept them long enough to be sufficiently cold he took them down and call'd for the Mulled Wine and they were very glad to set close to the Fire and leave Slaying for those who were too warm.

This I quote to execrate the memory of Mr. Houston and express my sympathy for his daughters.

There were no entertainments more popular, from the middle of the past century to the early years of this one, than "turtle frolics," what Burnaby called turtle-feasts. Every sea-captain who sailed to the West Indies intended and was expected to bring home a turtle on the return voyage; and if he were only to touch at the West Indies and thence pass on to more distant shores, he still tried, if possible, to secure a turtle and send it home by some returning vessel. In no seaport town did the turtle frolic come to a higher state of perfection than in Newport. Scores of turtles were borne to that welcoming shore. In 1752 George Bresett, a Newport gentleman, sailed to the West

Indies, and promptly did a neighborly and civic duty by sending home to his friend Samuel Freebody, a gallant turtle and a generous keg of limes. Lime juice was the fashionable and favorite "souring" of the day, to combine with arrack and Barbadoes rum into a glorious punch. The turtle arrived in prime condition, and Freebody handed the prize over to a slave-body named Cuffy Cockroach. He was a Guinea Coast negro, of a race who were (as I have noted before) the most intelligent of all the Africans brought as slaves to these shores. Any negro who acquired a position of dignity or trust or skill in this country, in colonial days, was sure to be a Guinea-boy. Cuffy Cockroach followed the rule, by filling a position of much dignity and trust and skill — as turtle-cook. He was a slave of Jaheel Brenton, but he cooked turtle for the entire town. The frolic was held at Fort George, on Goat Island, on December 23. The guests, fifty ladies and gentlemen, sailed over in a sloop, and were welcomed with hoisted flag and salute of cannon. The dinner was served at two, tea at five, and then dancing begun. *Pea Straw, Faithful Shep-*

herd, Arcadian Nuptials, were allemanded
and footed, and the keg of limes and its fel-
low-ingredients kept pace with the turtle.
The moon was at the full when the party
landed at the Newport wharf at eleven, but
the frolic was not ended. For instead of
the jolly crowd separating, they went the
rounds, leaving one member of the party at
a time at his own door, and then serenading
him or her, till the whole company had been
honored in succession. When Sammy wrote
to Mr. Bresett he said : —

Upon the whole the entertainment had the
preference over all turtle frolics before it, and Mr
George Bresetts health with "Honest George"
was freely drank in a cheerful glass by every person ; and at the request of the company I return
you their compliments for the foundation of so
agreeable an entertainment.

We find even so staid and dignified a minister and legislator as Manasseh Cutler writing thus in Providence in 1787 : —

This morning I received a polite invitation
from Govenor Bowen in the name of a large company to join them in a Turtle Frolic about six
miles out of town. Mr Hitchcock and other
clergymen of the town were of the party but

much against my inclination I was obliged to excuse myself.

The traveller who drives through the by-roads of New England to-day is almost ready to assert that there is no dwelling too poor or too lonely to contain a piano, or at the very least a melodeon or parlor organ. The sounds of Czerny's exercises issue from every farmhouse. There may be no new farm implements, no sewing-machine, but there will surely be a piano. This love of music has ever existed on those rock-bound shores, though in early days it found a stunted and sad expression in hymn tunes only, and the performance of music could scarce be called a colonial accomplishment. The first musical instruments were martial, drums and fifes and hautboys. I have never seen, in any personal inventory, the notice of a "gitterne" as in similar Virginian lists.

But in the early years of the eighteenth century a few spinets must have been exported to Boston and Philadelphia, and perhaps to Virginia. In 1712 an advertisement was placed in the *Boston News-Letter* that the Spinet would be taught, and on April 23, 1716, appeared in the same paper : —

Note that any Persons may have all Instruments of Music mended or Virginalls or Spinnets Strung & Tun'd, at a Reasonable Rate & likewise may be taught to play on any of the Instruments above mentioned.

In August, 1740, a "Good Spinnet" was offered for sale, and soon after a second-hand "Spinnet," and in January, 1750, "Spinnet wire."

On September 18, 1769, this notice appeared in the *Boston Gazette and Country Journal :* —

It is with pleasure that we inform the Public that a few days since was ship'd for Newport a very Curious Spinnet being the first ever made in America, the performance of the ingenious Mr. John Harris of Boston (son of the late Mr. Jos. Harris of London, Harpsichord and Spinnet Maker deceased) and in every respect does honor to that Artist who now carries on the Business at his house a few doors Northward of Dr. Clarkes, North End of Boston.

This first American spinet is said to be still in existence in a house in Newport on the corner of Thames and Gidley streets. It has one set of jacks and strings. The hammers have crow-quills which press on brass strings. It has ancient neighbors. In Bristol, R. I., is a triangular spinet four feet long, which is more than a century older than the town which is now its home. It bears this maker's mark, — "Johann Hitchcock fecit London 1520." If this date is correct, it is the oldest spinet known, the one of Italian manufacture in the British Museum being dated 1521.

At the rooms of the Essex Institute in Salem, Mass., is an old spinet made by Dr. Samuel Blyth in that town. Henry M. Brooks, Esq., author of *Olden Time Music*, has in his possession a bill for one of these American spinets that shows that the price in 1786 was £18. In the Memorial Hall at Deerfield, Mass., may be seen another dilapidated one, made by Stephanus & Keene. This belonged once to Mrs. Sukey Barker, of Hingham.

In the *Newport Mercury* of May 17, 1773, is advertised, "To be sold a Spinnet of a proper size for a little miss, and a most agreeable tone — plays extremely easy on the keys. Inquire of the Printer." Advertisement of the sale of spinets and of instruction on the spinet do not disappear from the newspapers in this country even after formidable rivals and successors, the harpsichord and forte-piano, had begun to be imported in comparatively large numbers.

The tone of a spinet has been characterized concisely by Holmes in his poem, *The Opening of the Piano,* — the "spinet with its thin metallic thrills." I know of nothing more truly the "relic of things that have passed away," more completely the voice of the past, than the tinkling thrill of a spinet. It is like seeing a ghost to touch the keys, and bring forth once more that obsolete sound. There is no sound born in the nineteenth century that at all resembles it. Like "loggerheads" in the coals and "lug-poles" in the chimney, like church lotteries and tithingmen, the spinet — even its very voice — is extinct.

Since in the *News-Letter* first quoted in this chapter virginals are named, I think the musical instrument of Queen Elizabeth must have been tolerably familiar to Bostonians. Judge Sewall, who "had a passion for music," writes in 1690 of fetching his wife's "virginalls." I cannot conceive what tunes Madam Sewall played on her virginals, no tawdry ballads and roundelays, no minuets and corams; she may have known half a dozen long-metre psalm tunes such as the Judge set for so many years in meeting.

"Forte-pianers" were imported to America, as were other musical instruments. It is said the first one brought to New England was in 1785 by John Brown for his daughter Sarah, afterwards Mrs. Herreshoff. It is still possessed by Miss Herreshoff, of Bristol, R. I. The first brought to "the Cape" was a Clementi of the date 1790, and found for many years a home in Falmouth. It is in perfect preservation, a dainty little inlaid box lying upon a slender low table, with tiny shelves for the music books, and a tiny little painted rack to hold the music sheets, and a pedal·fit for the foot of a doll. It is now owned by Miss Frances Morse, of Worcester, Mass. An old Broadwood piano, once owned by the venerable Dr. Sweetser, may be seen at the rooms of the Worcester Society of Antiquity; and still another, a Clementi, at the Essex Institute in Salem.

By the beginning of this century pianoplaying became a more common accomplishment, especially in the large towns, though

General Oliver said that in 1810, among the
six thousand families in Boston, there were
not fifty pianos. Rev. Manasseh Cutler
writes in 1801, from Washington, of a young
friend : —

She has been educated at the best schools in
Baltimore and Alexandria. She does not converse much, but is very modest and agreeable.
She plays with great skill on the Forte Piano
which she always accompanies with the most
delightful voice, and is frequently joined in the
vocal part by her mother. Mr. King has an excellent Forte-Piano which is connected with an
organ placed under it, which she plays and fills
with her feet, while her fingers are employed upon
the Forte-Piano. On Sunday evenings she constantly plays Psalm music. Miss Anna plays
Denmark remarkably well. But the most of the
psalm tunes our gentlemen prefer are the old
ones such as Old Hundred, Canterbury, which
you would be delighted to hear on the Forte-
Piano assisted by the Organ. Miss Anna gave
us some good music this evening, particularly the
Wayworn Traveller, Ma Chere Amie, The Tea,
The Twins of Latma (somewhat similar to Indian
Chief) Eliza, Lucy or Selims Complaint. These
are among my favourites.

In February, 1800, Eliza Southgate Bowne wrote thus in Boston : —

In the morning I am going to look at some Instruments ; however we got one picked out that I imagine we shall take, 150 dollars, a charming toned one and not made in this country.

In June she said enthusiastically of her "Instrument :" —

I am learning my 12th tune Oh Octavia, I almost worship my Instrument, — it reciprocates my joys and sorrows, and is my bosom companion. How I long to have you return! I have hardly attempted to sing since you went away. I am sure I shall not dare to when you return. I must enjoy my triumph while you are absent; my musical talents will be dim when compared with the lustre of yours.

The most universal accomplishment of colonial women was the making of samplers, if, indeed, anything could be termed an accomplishment which was so rigidly and prosaically part of their education. I can well imagine the disgrace it would have been to any little miss in her teens a century ago not to be able to show a carefully designed and wrought sampler. On these samplers were displayed the alphabet, sometimes in various

shaped letters — thus did she learn to mark
neatly her household linen ; bands of conven-
tional designs, of flowers, of geometrical pat-
terns — thus was she taught to embroider
muslin caps and kerchiefs ; and there were
gorgeous flowers and strange buildings, and
domestic scenes, and pastoral views, birds
that perched as large as cows, and roses that
were larger than either ; and last and best of
all (and often of much satisfaction to the
genealogist), there was her name and her age,
and sometimes her place of birth, and withal
a pious verse as a motto for this housewifely
shield. Of all the relics of old-time life
which have come to us, none are more interesting than the samplers. Happily, many of
them *have* come to us ; worked with wiry
enduring crewels and silk on strong linen
canvas, they speak down through the century of the little, useful, willing hands that
worked them ; of the tidy sempstresses and
housewives of those simple domestic days.
We know little of the daughters of the Pil-
grims, but Lora Standish has sent to us a
prim little message of her piety, and a faded
testimony of her skill, that makes her seem
dear to us : —

Lora Standish is My Name.
Lord Guide my heart that I may do thy Will
Also fill my hands with such convenient skill
As will conduce to Virtue void of Shame,
And I will give the Glory to Thy Name.

A more ambitious kind of needlework took
the form of what were known as mourning
pieces. These were regarded with deepest
affection, for were they not a token of loving remembrance? They bore stiff present-
ments of funeral urns, with drooping willows,
or a monument with a bowed and weeping
figure. Often the names of dead members
of the family were worked upon the monument. A still more ambitious sampler bore
a design known as The Tree of Life. A
stiffly branched tree was sparingly hung with
apples labelled with the names of the virtues
of humanity, such as Love, Honor, Truth,
Modesty, Silence. A white-winged angel on
one side of this tree watered the roots with
a very realistic watering-pot, and was bal-
anced with exactness, as were evenly adjusted
all good embroidery designs of that day, by
an inky-black Satan who bore a pitchfork of
colossal proportions and a tail as long as a
kite's, and so heavy that he could scarce have

dragged it along the ground — much less with it have flown.

For many years a favorite and much praised accomplishment was the cutting of paper in ornamental designs. This art was ambitiously called Papyrotamia, and it was of special usefulness in its application to watch-papers, a favorite lover's token of the day. The watch proper at that time was separate and removable from its case, which was of gold, silver, shagreen, or lacquer. Of course the watch did not fit closely into the case, and watch-papers were placed within to serve as a cushion to prevent jar and wear; sometimes the case would hold several. Artistic and grotesque taste could be used in the manufacture of these tokens of regard. I have seen them cut in various open-work designs from gilt and silver paper, embroidered in hair, painted in water colors. One I have has two turtle-doves billing over two hearts, and surrounded by a tiny wreath; another, embroidered on net, has the words "God is Love;" another has a moss rose and the words "Rejoice and blossom as a rose." Another bears a funeral urn, and is evidently *in memoriam*. Still another, a heart and arrows, and the sentimental legend "Kill me for I die of love." Jefferson, writing as a young man, bitterly deplores his inadvertent tearing of watch-papers which had been cut for him by his beloved Belinda. Watch and watch-papers had been accidentally soaked in water, and when he attempted to remove the papers, he says, "My cursed fingers gave them such a rent as I fear I shall never get over. I would have cried bitterly, but that I thought it beneath the dignity of a man." And he trusts the fair Becca will give him another paper of her cutting, which, though but a plain round one, he will esteem more than the nicest in the world cut by other hands.

Nothing can be more pathetic than the thoughtful survey of the crude and often cumbersome and ludicrous attempts at decorative art, through which the stunted and cramped love of the beautiful found expression, until our own day, in country homes. The dreary succession of hair-work, feather-work, wax flowers, shell-work, the crystallization with various domestic minerals and gums of dried leaves and grasses, vied with yarn and worsted monstrosities, and bewildering

patchwork. Occasionally some bold feminine spirit, made inventive through artistic
longing, gave birth to a novel, though too
often grotesque form of decoration.

A most interesting symbol of exquisite
neatness, unbounded patience, and blind
groping for artistic expression was Rhoda
Baker's "Leather-Works." Rhoda Baker
lived in a small Rhode Island village, which
was dull at its birth and slow of growth and
progress. She had a nature so timid, so
repelling, and so wholly introspective, that,
after nearly fifty years of shy and even unwilling "keeping company" with a preaching elder of the time, — a saint, almost a
mystic, — she died without ever having given
to the quaint, thin, pleasant-faced, awkward
man, one word of encouragement to his equally
timid, his hinting and halting love-making.
During those patient years of warm hopes,
but most scanty fruition, he had built a
house on an island which he owned in Narragansett Bay, with a window where his beloved Rhoda could sit sewing when she became his wife, and watch him happily rowing
across the Bay to her ; but great lilac bushes
grew up unchecked, and shaded and finally

hid the window at which Rhoda never sat to welcome her husband-lover. After her death the Elder so grieved that he had naught to remind him and speak to him of his beloved, that he boldly decided to name his boat for her; but as he could not conscientiously say she had ever encouraged him by word or look in his incipient love-making, and he must be strictly honest and chivalrously respectful to her memory, he painted upon the boat in black letters this truthful yet dimly consoling legend, " Rhoda Wouldnt." Poor Elder! Many a time had he ventured a-courting, and slowly entering, after his unanswered assault upon the door-knocker, had found the kitchen of this elusive Rhoda vacant, — *but her rocking-chair was slowly rocking*, — so he sadly left the deserted room, the unwelcoming house.

He sacrificed his life to his affection for his dead love. He had all his days a fear, a premonition, that he should lose his life through a horse, so he never rode or drove, but walked, rowed, or sailed, and lived on an island to escape his dreaded doom. When Rhoda's brother died in a distant town, the Elder was bidden to the funeral, and he

honored his Rhoda's memory by his attendance, and he had to ride there. As he left
the house of mourning, a fractious young
colt ran away with him, threw him out of the
wagon, and broke his neck.

His sweetheart's "Leather-Works" still
exist, to keep fresh this New England
romance. I saw them last summer in the
attic of the Town Hall. Rhoda left them in
her will to her church, and they are now the
property of the village church-guild. The
guild is vigorous and young, so can bear this
ancient maiden's bequest with cheerful carriage and undaunted spirits. The leather-
works are many and ponderous. One is
a vast trellis (which may have been originally two clothes-horses), hung with elabo-
rately twisted and tendrilled vines, bearing
minutely veined leaves and various counter-
feit and imaginary fruits. The bunches of
grapes are made of home-cast leaden bullets, or round stones, covered dexterously
and with unparalleled neatness and imper-
ceptible stitches with pieces of old kid gloves
or thin leather ; and to each a common dress-
hook is attached. The stem of the bunch
has corresponding eyes, to each of which a

grape is hung. By this ingenious means
the bunches of grapes could be neatly dusted
each week, and kept in repair, as well as easily shaped. On this trellis hung also Roses
of Sharon, a mystic flower which Rhoda's
sister Eunice invented, and which had a
deep spiritual signification, as well as extraordinary outline and intricate composition.
Every leaf, every grape, every monstrous
fruit, every flower of these Leather-Works,
speaks of the æsthetic longing, the vague
mysticism, the stifled repression, of Rhoda
Baker's life; and they speak equally of the
Elder's love. It was he who moulded the
bullets, and searched on the shore for carefully rounded stones; and he who haunted
the country saddlers and repair-shops for
waste strips of leather, which he often deposited in the silent kitchen by the rocking-
chair, sure of grateful though unspoken
thanks. Many a pair of his old boot-tops
figures as glorious vine leaves; and he
even tanned and dressed skins to supply
swiftly the artist's materials when genius
burned. It was he who tenderly unhooked
the grapes and pears, the fruits of Eden and
the Roses of Sharon, when the trellis was

transported to the Town Hall, and he rev-
erently placed the trophies of his true love's
skill and genius in place in their new home.
I always rather resent the fact that Rhoda
did not bequeath the Leather-Works to him,
when I think of the vast and almost sacred
pleasure he would have had in them; as well
as when I remember the share he had in the
preparations for their manufacture. And the
Leather-Works speak still another lesson,
as do many of the household grotesqueries
seen in New England, a lesson of sympathy,
almost of beauty, to those who "read
between the lines, the finer
grace of unfulfilled
designs."

CHAPTER X.

DAUGHTERS OF LIBERTY.

WE are constantly hearing the statement reiterated, that the Society of the Daughters of the American Revolution was the first association of women ever formed for patriotic purpose. This assertion shows a lamentable ignorance of Revolutionary history; for a century and a quarter ago, before the War of the Revolution, patriotic societies of women were formed all over the country, and called Daughters of Liberty. Our modern bands should be distinguished by being called the first patriotic-hereditary societies of women.

As we approach Revolutionary days, it is evident that the women of all the colonies were as deeply stirred as were the men at the constant injustice and growing tyranny of the British government, and they were not slow in openly averring their abhorrence and revolt against this injustice. Their individual action consisted in the wearing only of garments of homespun manufacture ; their concerted exertions in gathering in patriotic bands to spin, and the signing of compacts to drink no more of the taxed tea, that significant emblem of British injustice and American revolt.

The earliest definite notice of any gathering of Daughters of Liberty was in Providence in 1766, when seventeen young ladies met at the house of Deacon Ephraim Bowen and spun all day long for the public benefit, and assumed the name Daughters of Liberty. The next meeting the little band had so increased in numbers that it had to meet in the Court House. At about the same time another band of daughters gathered at Newport, and an old list of the members has been preserved. It comprised all the beautiful and brilliant young girls for which Newport was at that time so celebrated. As one result of this patriotic interest, the President and the first graduating class of Brown University, then called Rhode Island College, were clothed, at Commencement in 1769, in fabrics of American homespun manufacture.

The senior class of the previous year at Harvard had been similarly dressed.

These little bands of patriotic women gathered far and wide throughout New England. At one meeting seventy linen wheels were employed. In Newbury, Beverly, Rowley, Ipswich, spinning matches were held. Let me show how the day was spent. I quote from the *Boston News-Letter:* —

Rowley. A number of thirty-three respectable ladies of the town met at sunrise [this was in July] with their wheels to spend the day at the house of the Rev'd Jedidiah Jewell in the laudable design of a spinning match. At an hour before sunset, the ladies then appearing neatly dressed, principally in homespun, a polite and generous repast of American production was set for their entertainment, after which being present many spectators of both sexes, Mr. Jewell delivered a profitable discourse from Romans xii. 2 : Not slothful in business, fervent in spirit, serving the Lord.

You will never find matters of church and patriotism very far apart in New England ; so I learn that when they met in Ipswich the Daughters of Liberty were also entertained with a sermon. The Newbury patriots drank Liberty Tea, and listened to a sermon on the text Proverbs xxxi. 19. Another text used at one of these gatherings was from Exodus xxxv. 25 : "And all the women that were wise-hearted did spin with their hands."

The women of Virginia were early in the patriotic impulses, yet few proofs of their action or determination remain. In a Northern paper, the *Boston Evening Post* of January 31, 1770, we read this Toast to the Southerners : —

NEW TOASTS.

The patriotic ladies of Virginia, who have nobly distinguished themselves by appearing in the Manufactures of America, and may those of the Massachusetts be laudably ambitious of not being outdone by Virginians.

The wise and virtuous part of the Fair Sex in Boston and other Towns, who being at length sensible that by the consumption of Teas they are supporting the Commissioners & other Tools of Power, have voluntarily agreed not to give or receive any further Entertainments of that Kind, until those Creatures, together with the Boston Standing Army, are removed, and the Revenue Acts repealed.

May the disgrace which a late venal & corrupt Assembly has brought upon a Sister Colony, be wiped away by a Dissolution.

This is pretty plain language, but it could not be strange to the public ear, for ere this Boston women had been appealed to in the press upon this same subject.

In the *Massachusetts Gazette*, as early as November 9, 1767, these lines show the indignant and revolutionary spirit of the time:

> Young ladies in town and those that live round
> Let a friend at this season advise you.
> Since money's so scarce and times growing worse,
> Strange things may soon hap and surprise you.
> First then throw aside your high top knots of pride
> Wear none but your own country linen.
> Of economy boast. Let your pride be the most
> To show cloaths of your own make and spinning.
> What if homespun they say is not quite so gay
> As brocades, yet be not in a passion,
> For when once it is known this is much wore in town,
> One and all will cry out 'T is the fashion.
> And as one and all agree that you'll not married be
> To such as will wear London factory
> But at first sight refuse, till e'en such you do choose
> As encourage our own manufactory.

Soon these frequent appeals, and the influence of the public and earnest revolt of the Sons of Liberty, resulted in a public compact of Boston women. It is thus recorded in the Boston press : —

The *Boston Evening Post :* —

Monday, February 12, 1770.

The following agreement has lately been come into by upwards of 300 Mistresses of Families in this Town ; in which Number the Ladies of the highest rank and Influence, that could be waited upon in so short a Time, are included.

BOSTON, January 31, 1770.

At a time when our invaluable Rights and Privileges are attacked in an unconstitutional and most alarming Manner, and as we find we are reproached for not being so ready as could be desired, to lend our Assistance, we think it our Duty perfectly to concur with the true Friends of Liberty in all Measures they have taken to save this abused Country from Ruin and Slavery. And particularly, we join with the very respectable Body of Merchants and other Inhabitants of this Town, who met in Faneuil Hall the 23d of this Instant, in their Resolutions, totally to abstain from the Use of Tea ; And as the greatest Part of the Revenue arising by Virtue of the late Acts, is produced from the Duty paid upon Tea, which Revenue is wholly expended to support the American Board of Com-

missioners ; We, the Subscribers, do strictly engage, that we will totally abstain from the Use of
that Article, (Sickness excepted) not only in our
respective Families, but that we will absolutely
refuse it, if it should be offered to us upon any
Occasion whatsoever. This Agreement we cheerfully come into, as we believe the very distressed
Situation of our Country requires it, and we do
hereby oblige ourselves religiously to observe it,
till the late Revenue Acts are repealed.

Massachusetts Gazette, and the *Boston
Weekly News-Letter :* —

February 15, 1770.

We hear that a large Number of the Mistresses
of Families, some of whom are Ladies of the
highest Rank, in this Town, have signed an
Agreement against drinking Tea (Bohea it is
supposed, tho' not specified) ; they engage not
only to abstain from it in their Families (Sickness excepted) but will absolutely refuse it, if it
should be offered to them upon any Occasion ;
This Agreement to be religiously observed till
the Revenue Acts are repealed.

It was natural that, in that hotbed of rebellion, young girls should not be behind
their brothers, fathers, and their mothers in
open avowal of their revolt. Soon the young
ladies published this declaration : —

We, the daughters of those patriots who have and do now appear for the public interest, and in that principally regard their posterity — as such, do with pleasure engage with them in denying ourselves the drinking of foreign tea in hopes to frustrate a plan which tends to deprive the whole community of all that is valuable as life.

One dame thus declared her principles and motives in blank verse : —

> Farewell the teaboard with its gaudy equipage
> Of cups and saucers, creambucket, sugar tongs,
> The pretty tea-chest, also lately stored
> With Hyson, Congo and best double-fine.
> Full many a joyous moment have I sat by ye
> Hearing the girls tattle, the old maids talk scandal,
> And the spruce coxcomb laugh at — maybe — nothing.
> Though now detestable
> Because I am taught (and I believe it true)
> Its use will fasten slavish chains upon my country
> To reign triumphant in America.

When little Anna Green Winslow bought a hat in February, 1771, she bought one of " white holland with the feathers sewed on in a most curious manner, white and unsulleyed as the falling snow. As I am as we say a daughter of Liberty I chuse to wear as much of our own manufactory as posible."

Mercy Warren wrote to John Winthrop, in fine satire upon this determination of American women to give up all imports from Great Britain except the necessaries of life, a list of the articles a woman would deem it imperative to retain : —

> An inventory clear
> Of all she needs Lamira offers here.
> Nor does she fear a rigid Catos frown
> When she lays by the rich embroidered gown
> And modestly compounds for just enough —
> Perhaps some dozen of more slighty stuff.
> With lawns and lutestrings, blond and mecklin laces,
> Fringes and jewels, fans and tweezer cases,
> Gay cloaks and hats of every shape and size,
> Scrafs, cardinals and ribbons of all dyes.
> With ruffles stamped, and aprons of tambour,
> Tippets and handkerchiefs at least three score ;
> With finest muslins that far India boasts,
> And the choice herbage from Chinesan coast.
> (But while the fragrant hyson leaf regales
> Who 'll wear the home-spun produce of the vales ?
> For if 't would save the nation from the curse
> Of standing troops — or name a plague still worse,
> Few can this choice delicious draught give up,
> Though all Medea's poison fill the cup.)
> Add feathers, furs, rich satins and ducapes
> And head dresses in pyramidal shapes,
> Sideboards of plate and porcelain profuse,
> With fifty dittos that the ladies use.
> So weak Lamira and her wants are few,
> Who can refuse, they 're but the sex 's due.

In youth indeed an antiquated page
Taught us the threatening of a Hebrew page
Gainst wimples, mantles, curls and crisping pins,
But rank not these among our modern sins,
For when our manners are well understood
What in the scale is stomacher or hood?
Tis true we love the courtly mien and air
The pride of dress and all the debonair,
Yet Clara quits the more dressed negligé
And substitutes the careless polanê
Until some fair one from Britannia's court
Some jaunty dress or newer taste import,
This sweet temptation could not be withstood,
Though for her purchase paid her father's blood.

After the war had really begun, Mrs. John Adams, writing July 31, 1777, tells of an astonishing action of Boston women, plainly the result of all these revolutionary tea-notions : —

There is a great scarcity of sugar and coffee, articles which the female part of the State is very loath to give up, especially whilst they consider the scarcity occasioned by the merchants having secreted a large quantity. There had been much rout and noise in the town for several weeks. Some stores had been opened by a number of people, and the coffee and sugar carried into the market and dealt out by pounds. It was rumored that an eminent stingy wealthy merchant (who is a bachelor) had a hogshead of coffee in his store

which he refused to sell the committee under six
shillings per pound. A number of females, some
say a hundred, some say more, assembled with a
cart and trunks, marched down to the warehouse
and demanded the keys which he refused to deliver. Upon which one of them seized him by
his neck and tossed him into the cart. Upon
his finding no quarter, he delivered the keys
when they tipped up the cart and discharged
him ; then opened the warehouse, hoisted out
the coffee themselves, put into the trunks, and
drove off. It was reported that he had personal
chastisements among them, but this I believe
was not true. A large concourse of men stood
amazed, silent spectators of the whole trans-
action.

I suppose these Boston dames thought
they might have coffee since they could not
have tea ; and, indeed, the relative use of
these two articles in America was much
changed by the Revolution. To this day
much more coffee is drunk in America, pro-
portionately, than in England. We are not
a tea-drinking nation.

I don't know that there were Daughters
of Liberty in Philadelphia, but Philadelphia
women were just as patriotic as those of other

towns. One wrote to a British officer as follows : —

I have retrenched every superfluous expense in my table and family. Tea I have not drunk since last Christmas, nor have I bought a cap or gown since your defeat at Lexington. I have learned to knit and am now making stockings of wool for my servants. In this way do I now throw in my mite for public good. I know this, that as free I can die but once, but as a slave I shall not be worthy of life. I have the pleasure to assure you that these are the sentiments of my sister Americans.

The women of the South were fired with patriotism ; in Mecklenburgh and Rowan counties, North Carolina, Daughters of Liberty found another method of spurring patriotism. Young ladies of the most respectable families banded together, and pledged themselves not to receive addresses from any recreant suitors who had not obeyed the country's call for military service.

There was an historic tea-party also in that town of so much importance in those days — Edenton, N. C. On October 25, 1774, fifty-one spirited dames assembled at the residence of Mrs. Elizabeth King, and passed resolutions commending the action of the Provincial Congress, and declared also that they would not conform to "that Pernicious Custom of Drinking Tea or that the aforesaid Ladys would not promote ye wear of any manufacture from England," until the tax was repealed.

The notice of the association is contained in the American Archives, and runs thus : —

Association Signed by Ladies of Edenton, North Carolina, Oct. 25, 1774. As we cannot be indifferent on any occasion that appears to affect the peace and happiness of our country, and as it has been thought necessary for the publick good to enter into several particular resolves, by meeting of Members of Deputies from the whole Province, it is a duty that we owe not only to our near and dear relations and connections, but to ourselves who are essentially interested in their welfare, to do everything as far as lies in our power to testify our sincere adherence to the same, and we do therefore accordingly subscribe this paper as a witness of our fixed intentions and solemn determination to do so. Signed by fifty one ladies.

It is a good example of the strange notions which some historians have of the slight value of circumstantial evidence in history, that the names of these fifty-one ladies have not been preserved. A few, however, are known. The president was Mrs. Penelope Barker, who was thrice a widow, of husbands Hodgson, Crumm, and Barker. She was high-spirited, and from her varied matrimonial experiences knew that it was needless to be afraid of any man; so when British soldiers invaded her stables to seize her carriage horses, she snatched the sword of one of her husbands from the wall, with a single blow severed the reins in the British officer's hands, and drove her horses back into the stables, and kept them too.

The fame of this Southern tea-party reached England, for Arthur Iredell wrote (with the usual masculine jocularity upon feminine enterprises) thus, on January 31, 1775, from London to his patriot brother, James Iredell:—

I see by the newspapers the Edenton ladies have signalized themselves by their protest against tea-drinking. The name of Johnston I see among others; are any of my sister's relations patriotic heroines? Is there a female Congress at Edenton too? I hope not, for we Englishmen are afraid of the male Congress, but if the ladies who have ever, since the Amazonian era, been esteemed the most formidable enemies, if they, I say, should attack us, the most fatal consequence is to be dreaded. So dextrous in the handling of a dart, each wound they give is mortal; whilst we, so unhappily formed by Nature, the more we strive to conquer them the more are conquered! The Edenton ladies, conscious I suppose of this superiority on their side, by former experience, are willing, I imagine, to crush us into atoms by their omnipotency; the only security on our side to prevent the impending ruin that I can perceive is the probability that there are few places in America which possess so much female artillery as in Edenton.

Another indication of the fame of the Edenton tea-party is adduced by Dr. Richard Dillard in his interesting magazine paper thereon. It was rendered more public by a caricature, printed in London, a mezzotint, entitled "A Society of Patriotic Ladies at Edenton in North Carolina." One lady with a gavel is evidently a man in woman's clothing, and is probably intended for the hated Lord North; other figures are pouring the tea out of caddies, others are writing. This caricature may have been brought forth in derision of an interesting tea-party picture which still exists, and is in North Carolina, after some strange vicissitudes in a foreign land. It is painted on glass, and the various figures are doubtless portraits of the Edenton ladies.

It is difficult to-day to be wholly sensible of all that these Liberty Bands meant to the women of the day. There were not, at that time, the associations of women for concerted charitable and philanthropic work which are so universal now. There were few established and organized assemblies of women for church work (there had been some praying-meetings in Whitefield's day), and the very thought of a woman's society for any other than religious purposes must have been in itself revolutionary. And we scarcely appreciate all it meant for them to abandon the use of tea; for tea-drinking in that day meant far more to women than it does now. Substitutes for the taxed and abandoned exotic herb were eagerly sought and speedily offered. Liberty Tea, Labrador Tea, and Yeopon were the most universally accepted, though seventeen different herbs and beans were named by one author; and patriotic prophecies were made that their use would wholly outlive that of the Oriental drink, even could the latter be freely obtained. A century has proved the value of these prophecies.

Liberty Tea was the most popular of these Revolutionary substitutes. It sold for six-pence a pound. It was made from the four-leaved loose-strife, a common-growing herb. It was pulled up whole like flax, its stalks were stripped of the leaves and then boiled. The leaves were put in a kettle with the liquor from the stalks and again boiled. Then the leaves were dried in an oven. Sage and rib-wort, strawberry leaves and currant leaves, made a shift to serve as tea. Hyperion or Labrador Tea, much vaunted, was only raspberry leaves, but was not such a wholly odious beverage. It was loudly praised in the patriotic public press : —

The use of Hyperion or Labrador tea is every day coming into vogue among people of all ranks. The virtues of the plant or shrub from which this delicate Tea is gathered were first discovered by the Aborigines, and from them the Canadians learned them. Before the cession of Canada to

Great Britain we knew little or nothing of this
most excellent herb, but since we have been
taught to find it growing all over hill and dale
between the Lat. 40 and 60. It is found all over
New England in great plenty and that
of best quality, particularly on the
banks of the Penobscot, Ken-
nebec, Nichewannock and
Merrimac.

CHAPTER XI.

A REVOLUTIONARY HOUSEWIFE.

WE do not need to make a composite picture of the housewife of Revolutionary days, for a very distinct account has been preserved of one in the quaint pages of the *Remembrancer* or diary of Christopher Marshall, a well-to-do Quaker of Philadelphia, who was one of the Committee of Observation of that city during the Revolutionary War. After many entries through the year 1778, which incidentally show the many cares of his faithful wife, and her fulfilment of these cares, the fortunate husband thus bursts forth in her praise : —

As I have in this memorandum taken scarcely any notice of my wife's employments, it might appear as if her engagements were very trifling ; the which is not the case but the reverse. And to do her justice which her services deserved, by entering them minutely, would take up most of my time, for this genuine reason, how that from

early in the morning till late at night she is constantly employed in the affairs of the family,
which for four months has been very large ; for
besides the addition to our family in the house,
it is a constant resort of comers and goers which
seldom go away with dry lips and hungry bellies.
This calls for her constant attendance, not only
to provide, but also to attend at getting prepared
in the kitchen, baking our bread and pies, meat
&c. and also the table. Her cleanliness about
the house, her attendance in the orchard, cutting
and drying apples of which several bushels have
been procured ; add to which her making of
cider without tools, for the constant drink of the
family, her seeing all our washing done, and her
fine clothes and my shirts, the which are all
smoothed by her ; add to this, her making of
twenty large cheeses, and that from one cow,
and daily using with milk and cream, besides
her sewing, knitting &c. Thus she looketh well
to the ways of her household, and eateth not the
bread of idleness ; yea she also stretcheth out
her hand, and she reacheth forth her hand to
her needy friends and neighbors. I think she
has not been above four times since her residence here to visit her neighbors ; nor through
mercy has she been sick for any time, but has at
all times been ready in any affliction to me or my

family as a faithful nurse and attendant both day and night.

Such laudatory references to the goodwife as these abound through the *Remembrancer.*

My tender wife keeps busily engaged and looks upon every Philadelphian who comes to us as a person suffering in a righteous cause ; and entitled to partake of her hospitality which she administers with her labor and attendance with great freedom and alacrity. . . .

My dear wife meets little respite all the day, the proverb being verified, that Woman's Work is never done.

I owe my health to the vigilance, industry and care of my wife who really has been and is a blessing unto me. For the constant assiduity and press of her daily and painful labor in the kitchen, the Great Lord of the Household will reward her in due time.

It seems that so generous and noble a woman should have had a reward in this world, as well as the next, for, besides her kitchen duties, she was a " nonsuch gardner, working bravely in her garden," and a first class butter-maker, who constantly supplied her poor neighbors with milk, and yet always had cream to spare for her dairy.

Far be it from me to cast even the slight-
est reflection, to express the vaguest doubt,
as to the industry, energy, and application of
so pious, so estimable an old gentleman as
Mr. Marshall, but he was, as he says, "easily
tired" — "the little I do tires and fatigues
me" — "the grasshopper seems a burden."
So, even to our prosaic and somewhat eman-
cipated nineteenth century notions as to
women's rights and their assumption of
men's duties, it does appear that so patient,
industrious, and overworked a consort might
have been spared some of the burdensome
duties which devolved upon her, and which
are popularly supposed not to belong to the
distaff side of the house. An elderly milk-
man might have occasionally milked the
cow for that elderly weary milkmaid. And
it does seem just a little strange that a
hearty old fellow, who could eat gammons
and drink punch at every occasion of sober
enjoyment and innocent revelry to which he
was invited, should let his aged spouse rise
at daybreak and go to the wharves to buy
loads of wood from the bargemen ; and also
complacently record that the horse would
have died had not the ever-energetic wife

gone out and by dint of hard work and good
management succeeded in buying in the
barren city a load of hay for provender.
However, he never fails to do her justice in
commendatory words in the pages of his
Remembrancer, thus proving himself more
thoughtful than that Yankee husband who
said to a neighbor that his wife was such a
good worker and a good cook, and so pleasant and kept everything so neat and nice
around the house, that sometimes it seemed
as if he could n't help telling her so.

One of the important housewifely cares of
Philadelphia women was their marketing,
and Madam Marshall was faithful in this
duty also. We find her attending market as
early as four o'clock upon a winter's morning.
In 1690, there were two market days weekly
in Philadelphia, and nearly all the early writers note the attendance thereat of the ladies
residing in the town. In 1744, these markets
were held on Tuesday and Friday. William
Black, a travelling Virginian, wrote that year
with admiration of this custom : —

I got to the market by 7, and had no small
Satisfaction in seeing the pretty Creatures, the

Young Ladies, traversing the place from Stall to Stall where they could make the best Market, some with their maid behind them with a Basket to carry home the Purchase, others that were design'd to buy but trifles, as a little fresh Butter, a Dish of Green Peas or the like, had Good Nature & Humility enough to be their own Porters. I have so much regard for the fair Sex that I imagin'd like the Woman of the Holy Writ some charm in touching even the Hem of their Garments. After I made my Market, which was one pennyworth of Whey and a Nosegay, I disengag'd myself.

It would appear also that a simple and appropriate garment was donned for this homely occupation. We find Sarah Eve and others writing of wearing a "market cloke."

It is with a keen thrill of sympathy that we read of all the torment that Mistress Marshall, that household saint, had to endure in the domestic service rendered to her — or perhaps I should say through the lack of service in her home. A special thorn in the flesh was one Poll, a bound girl. On September 13, 1775, Mr. Marshall wrote : —

After my wife came from market (she went past 5) she ordered her girl Poll to carry the basket with some necessaries to the place, as she was coming after her, they intending to iron the clothes. Poll accordingly went, set down the basket, came back, went and dressed herself all clean, short calico gown, and said she was going to school; but presently after the negro woman Dinah came to look for her, her mistress having mistrusted she had a mind to play truant. This was about nine, but madam took her walk, but where — she is not come back to tell.

Sept. 16. I arose before six as I was much concern'd to see my wife so afflicted as before on the bad conduct of her girl Poll who is not yet returned, but is skulking and running about town. This I understand was the practice of her mother who for many years before her death was a constant plague to my wife, and who left her this girl as a legacy, and who by report as well as by own knowledge, for almost three years has always been so down to this time. About eight, word was brought that Poll was just taken by Sister Lynn near the market, and brought to their house. A messenger was immediately dispatched for her, as she could not be found before, though a number of times they had been hunting her.

As the years went on, Poll kept taking what he called "cruises," "driving strokes of impudence," visiting friends, strolling around the streets, faring up and down the country, and he patiently writes : —

This night our girl was brought home. I suppose she was hunted out, as it is called, and found by Ruth on the Passyunk Road. Her mistress was delighted upon her return, but I know of nobody else in house or out. I have nothing to say in the affair, as I know of nothing that would distress my wife so much as for me to refuse or forbid her being taken into the house.

(A short time after) I arose by four as my wife had been up sometime at work cleaning house, and as she could not rest on account of Polls not being yet return'd. The girls frolics always afflict her mistress, so that to me its plain if she does not mend, or her mistress grieve less for her, that it will shorten Mrs Marshalls days considerably ; besides our house wears quite a different face when Miss Poll is in it (although all the good she does is not worth half the salt she eats.) As her presence gives pleasure to her mistress, this gives joy to all the house, so that in fact she is the cause of peace or uneasiness in the home.

It is with a feeling of malicious satisfaction that we read at last of the jaded, harassed, and conscientious wife going away for a visit, and know that the man of the house

will have to encounter and adjust domestic
problems as best he may. No sooner had
the mistress gone than Poll promptly departed also on a vacation. As scores of
times before, Mr. Marshall searched for her,
and retrieved her (when she was ready to
come), and she behaved exceeding well for a
day, only, when rested, to again make a flit-
ting. He writes on the 23d : —

I roused Charles up at daylight. Found Miss
Poll in the straw house. She came into the
kitchen and talked away that she could not go
out at night but she must be locked out. If that's
the case she told them she would pack up her
clothes and go quite away ; that she would not be
so served as her Mistress did not hinder her stay-
ing out when she pleased, and the kitchen door
to be opened for her when she came home and
knocked. The negro woman told me as well as
she could what she said. I then went and picked
up her clothes that I could find. I asked her
how she could behave so to me when I had conducted myself so easy towards her even so as to
suffer her to sit at table and eat with me. This
had no effect upon her. She rather inclined to
think that she had not offended and had done
nothing but what her mistress indulged her in.
I told her before Betty that it was not worth my

while to lick her though she really deserved it for her present impudence; but to remember I had taken all her clothes I could find except what she had on, which I intended to keep; that if she went away Charles with the horse should follow her and bring her back and that I would send a bellman around the borough of Lancaster to cry her as a runaway servant, wicked girl, with a reward for apprehending her.

The fatuous simplicity of Quaker Marshall's reproofs, the futility of his threats, the absurd failure of his masculine methods, received immediate illustration — as might be expected, by Miss Poll promptly running away that very night. Again he writes : —

Charles arose near daybreak and I soon after, in order to try to find my nightly and daily plague, as she took a walk again last night. Charles found her. We turned her upstairs to refresh herself with sleep. . . .

(Two days later) After breakfast let our Poll downstairs where she has been kept since her last frolic. Fastened her up again at night. I think my old enemy Satan is much concerned in the conduct and behavior of that unfortunate girl. He knows her actions give me much anxiety and indeed at times raise my anger so I have said what should have been avoided, but I hope for the future to be more upon my guard and thus frustrate him in his attempts.

With what joy did the masculine house-keeper and steward greet the return of his capable wife, and resign his position as turn-key! Poll, upon liberation from restraint, flew swiftly away like any other bird from its cage.

Notwithstanding such heavy weather overhead and exceeding dirty under foot our Poll after breakfast went to see the soldiers that came as prisoners belonging to Burgoynes army. Our trull returned this morning. Her mistress gave her a good sound whipping. This latter was a variety.

And so the unequal fight went on; Poll calmly breaking down a portion of the fence that she might decamp more promptly, and return unheralded. She does not seem to have been vicious, but simply triumphantly lawless and fond of gadding. I cannot always blame her. I am sure I should have wanted to go to see the soldier-prisoners of Burgoyne's army brought into town. The last glimpse of her we have is with "her head dressed in tiptop fashion," rolling off in a coach to Yorktown with Sam Morris's son, and not even saying good-by to her vanquished master.

Mr. Marshall was not the only Philadelphian to be thus afflicted; we find one of his neighbors, Jacob Hiltzheimer, dealing a more summary way with a refractory maid-servant. Shortly after noting in the pages of his diary that "our maid Rosina was impertinent to her mistress," we find this good citizen taking the saucy young redemptioner before the squire, who summarily ordered her to the workhouse. After remaining a month in that confinement, Rosina boldly answered no, when asked if she would go back to her master and behave as she ought, and she was promptly remanded. But she soon repented, and was released. Her master paid for her board and lodging while under detention, and quickly sold her for £20 for her remaining term of service.

With the flight of the Marshalls' sorry Poll, the sorrows and trials of this good Quaker household with regard to what Raleigh calls "domesticals" were not at an end. As the "creatures" and the orchard and garden needed such constant attention, a man-servant was engaged — one Antony — a character worthy of Shakespeare's comedies. Soon we find the master writing : —

I arose past seven and had our gentleman to call down stairs. I spoke to him about his not serving the cows. He at once began about his way being all right, &c. I set about serving our family and let him, as in common, do as he pleases. I think I have hired a plague to my spirit. Yet he is still the same Antony — he says — complaisant, careful, cheerful, industrious.

Then Antony grew noisy and talkative, so abusive at last that he had to be put out in the yard, where he railed and talked till midnight, to the annoyance of the neighbors and the mortification of his mistress; for he protested incessantly and noisily that all he wished was to leave in peace and quiet, which he was not permitted to do. Then, and repeatedly, his master told him to leave, but the servant had no other home, and might starve in the war-desolated town ; so after half-promises he was allowed by these tender folk to stay on. Soon he had another "tantrum," and the astounded Quaker writes : —

He rages terribly uttering the most out of the way wicked expressions yet not down-right swearing. Mamma says it is cursing in the Popish way. . . .

What this Popish swearing could have been arouses my curiosity; I suspect it was a kind of "dog-latin." Antony constantly indulged in it, to the horror and sorrow of the pious Marshalls. And the amusing, the fairly comic side of all this is that Antony was a preacher, a prophet in the land, and constantly held forth in meeting to sinners around him. We read of him : —

Antony went to Quakers meeting today where he preached; although he was requested to desist, so that by consent they broke up the meeting sooner than they would have done. . . .

Mamma went to meeting where Antony spoke and was forbid. He appeared to be most consummately bold and ignorant in his speaking there. And about the house I am obliged in a stern manner at times to order him not to say one word more. . . .

This afternoon Antony preached at the English Presbyterian meeting. It is said that the hearers laughed at him but he was highly pleased with himself.

Antony preached at meeting. I kept engaged
helping to cook the pot against master came
home. He comes and goes as he pleases.

I don't know when to pity poor Dame
Marshall the most, with Antony railing in
the yard and disturbing the peace of the
neighbors; or Antony cursing in a Popish
manner through the house; or Antony sham-
ming sick and moaning by the fireside; or
Antony violently preaching when she had
gone to the quiet Quaker meeting for an
hour of peace and rest.

This "runnagate rascal" was as elusive,
as tricky, as malicious as a gnome; whenever he was reproved, he always contrived
to invent a new method of annoyance in
revenge. When chidden for not feeding the
horse, he at once stripped the leaves off the
growing cabbages, cut off the carrot heads,
and pulled up the potatoes, and pretended
and protested he did it all solely to benefit them, and thus do good to his master.
When asked to milk the cow, he promptly
left the Marshall domicile for a whole day.

Sent Antony in the orchard to watch the boys.
As I was doubtful sometime whether if any came

for apples Antony would prevent, I took a walk to the back fence, made a noise by pounding as if I would break the fence, with other noise. This convinced me Antony sat in his chair. He took no notice till my wife and old Rachel came to him, roused him, and scolded him for his neglect. His answer was that he thought it his duty to be still and not disturb them, as by so doing he should have peace in heaven and a blessing would ever attend him.

This was certainly the most sanctimonious excuse for laziness that was ever invented ; and on the following day Antony supplemented his tergiversation by giving away all Mr. Marshall's ripe apples through the fence to passers-by — neighbors, boys, soldiers, and prisoners. There may have been method in this orchard madness, for Antony loathed apple-pie, a frequent comestible in the Marshall domicile, and often refused to drink cider, and grumbling made toast-tea instead. In a triumph of euphuistic indignation, Mr. Marshall thus records the dietetic vagaries of the " most lazy impertinent talking lying fellow any family was ever troubled with : "

When we have no fresh broth he wants some ; when we have it he cant sup it. When we have lean of bacon he wants the fat ; when the fat he cant eat it without spreading salt over it as without it its too heavy for his stomach. If new milk he cant eat it till its sour, it curdles on his stomach ; when sour or bonnyclabber it gives him the stomach-ache. Give him tea he doesn't like such slop, its not fit for working men ; if he hasn't it when he asks for it he's not well used. Give him apple pie above once for some days, its not suitable for him it makes him sick. If the negro woman makes his bed, she dont make it right ; if she dont make it she's a lazy black jade, &c.

In revenge upon the negro woman Dinah for not making his bed to suit his notion, he pretended to have had a dream about her, which he interpreted to such telling effect that she thought Satan was on his swift way to secure her, and fled the house in superstitious fright, in petticoat and shift, and was captured three miles out of town. On her return, Antony outdid himself with "all the vile ribaldry, papist swearing, incoherent scurrilous language, that imperious pride, vanity, and folly could invent or express" — and then went off to meeting to preach and pray. Well might the Quaker say with Juvenal, " The tongue is the worst part of a bad servant." At last, exasperated beyond measure, his patient master vowed, "Antony, I will give thee a good whipping," and he could do it, for he had "pacified himself with sundry stripes of the cowskin" on Dinah, the negro, when she, in emulation of Antony, was impertinent to her mistress.

The threat of a whipping brought on Antony a "fit of stillness" which descended like a blessing on the exhausted house. But " the devil is sooner raised than laid ; " anon Antony was in his old lunes again, and the peace was broken by a fresh outburst of laziness, indifference, and abuse, in which we must leave this afflicted household, for at that date the *Remembrancer* abruptly closes.

The only truly good service rendered to those much tried souls was by a negro woman, Dinah, who, too good for this earth, died ; and in her death involved them in fresh trouble, for in that war-swept town they could scarce procure her burial.

CHAPTER XII.

FIRESIDE INDUSTRIES.

AROUND the great glowing fireplace in
an old New England kitchen centred
the homeliness and picturesqueness of an old-
time home. The walls and floor were bare;
the furniture was often meagre, plain, and
comfortless; the windows were small and ill-
fitting; the whole house was draughty and
cold; but in the kitchen glowed a benefi-
cent heart that spread warmth and cheer and
welcome, and beauty also when

> the old rude-furnished room
> Burst flower-like into rosy bloom.

The settlers builded great chimneys with
ample open hearths, and to those hearths
the vast forests supplied plentiful fuel; but
as the forests disappeared in the vicinity of
the towns, the fireplaces also shrank in size,
so that in Franklin's day he could write of
the big chimneys as "the fireplaces of our
fathers;" and his inventions for economiz-

ing fuel had begun to be regarded as necessities.

The kitchen was the housewife's domain, the chimney-seat her throne; but the furniture of that throne and the sceptre were far different from the kitchen furnishings of to-day.

We often see fireplaces with hanging cranes in pictures illustrating earliest colonial times, but the crane was unknown in those days. When the seventeenth-century chimney was built, ledges were left on either side, and on them rested the ends of a long heavy pole of green wood, called a lug-pole or back bar. The derivation of the word lug-pole is often given as meaning from lug to lug, as the chimney-side was often called the lug. Whittier wrote:—

And for him who sat by the chimney lug.

Others give it from the old English word *lug*, to carry; for it was indeed the carrying-pole. It was placed high up in the yawning chimney, with the thought and intent of its being out of reach of the devouring flames, and from it hung a motley collection of hooks of various lengths and weights, sometimes with long rods, sometimes with chains, and rejoicing in various names. Pot-hooks, pot - hangers, pot - hangles, pot - claws, pot-cleps, were one and the same; so also were trammels and crooks. Gib and gibcroke were other titles. Hake was of course the old English for hook :—

> On went the boilers till the hake
> Had much ado to bear 'em.

A twi-crook was a double hook.

Other terms were gallow-balke, for the lug-pole, and gallow-crookes for pot-hooks. These were Yorkshire words, used alike in that county by common folk and gentry. They appear in the inventory of the goods of Sir Timothy Hutton, and in the farming-book of Henry Best, both dating to the time of settlement of New England. A recon was another Yorkshire name for a chain with pot-hooks. They were heard but rarely in New England.

The "eetch-hooke" named by Thomas Angell, of Providence, in 1694, with his "tramils and pot hookes" is an unknown and undescribable form of trammel to me, possibly an H-hook.

By these vari-named hooks were suspended at various heights over the flames pots, kettles, and other bailed cooking utensils.

The lug-pole, though made of green wood, often became brittle or charred through too long and careless use over the hot fire, and was left in the chimney till it broke under its weighty burden of food and metal. And as within the chimney corner was a favorite seat for both old and young of the household, not only were precious cooking utensils endangered and food lost, but human life as well, as told in Judge Sewall's diary, and in other diaries and letters of the times. So, when the iron crane was hung in the fireplace, it not only added grace and convenience to the family hearth, but safety as well. On it still were hung the pot-hooks and trammels, but with shortened arms or hangers.

The mantel was sometimes called by the old English name, clavy or clavel-piece. In one of John Wynter's letters, written in 1634, he describes his new home in Maine :

The chimney is large, with an oven in each end of him : he is so large that we can place our Cyttle within the Clavell-piece. We can brew and bake and boyl our Cyttle all at once in him.

The change in methods of cooking is plainly evinced in many of our common kitchen utensils. In olden times the pots and kettles always stood on legs, and all skillets and frying-pans and saucepans stood on slender legs, that, if desired, they might be placed with their contents over small beds of coals raked to one side of the hearth. A further convenience to assist this standing over coals was a little trivet, a tripod or three-footed stand, usually but a simple skeleton frame on which the skillet could be placed. In the corner of a fireplace would be seen trivets with legs of various lengths, through which the desired amount of heat could be obtained. We read in Eden's *First Books on America:* —

He shulde fynde in one place a fryingpan, in another chauldron, here a tryvet, there a spytte, and these in kynde in every pore mans house : —

Of somewhat later date was the toast rack, also standing on its little spindling legs.

No better list can be given of the kitchen utensils of earliest colonial days in America

than those found in the inventories of the
estates of the dead immigrants. These inventories are, in some cases, still preserved
in the Colonial Court Records. We find
that Madam Olmstead, of Hartford, Conn.,
had, in 1640, in her kitchen : —

2 Brasse Skillets 1 Ladle 1 candlestick
one mortar all of brasse 1 brasse pott 5.

7 Small peuter dishes 1 peuter bason 6
porringers 2 peuter candlesticks 1
frudishe 2 little sasers 1 smale plate. 1. 10.

7 biger peuter dishes 1 salt 2 peuter
cupps 1 peuter dram 1 peuter bottel
1 Warmeing pan 13 peuter spoons... 2. 12.

1 Stupan 3 bowles & a tunnel 7 dishes
10 spoones one Wooddin cupp 1
Wooddin platter with three old latten
panns Two dozen and a halfe trenchers two wyer candlesticks.......... 11.

2 Jacks 2 Bottels 2 drinking hornes 1
little pott........................ 10.

2 beare hogsheads 2 beare barrels 2
powdering tubs 4 brueing vessels 1
cowle 2 firkins.................... 2.

This was certainly a very good outfit. The
utensils for the manufacture and storage of
beer did not probably stand in the kitchen,

but in the lean-to or brew-house. A "cowl" was a large tub with ears; in it liquids could be carried by two persons, who bore the ends of a pole thrust through the ears or handles. Often with the cowl was specified a pail with iron bail. William Harris, of Pawtuxet, R. I., had, in 1681, "two Payles and one jron Bayle" worth three shillings. This naming of the pail-bail marked the change in the form of pail handles; originally, pails were carried by sticks thrust through ears on either side of the vessel.

The jacks were waxed leather jugs or drinking horns, much used in English ale-houses in the fourteenth and fifteenth centuries, whose use gave rise to the singular notion of the French that Englishmen drank their ale out of their boots. Governor Winthrop had jacks and leather bottles; but both names disappear from inventories by the year 1700, in New England.

These leather bottles were in universal use in England "among shepherds and harvest-people in the countrey." They were also called bombards. Their praises were sung in a very spirited ballad, of which I give a few lines : —

I wish in heaven his soul may dwell
Who first found out the leather bottell.
A leather bottell we know is good
Far better than glasses or cases of wood,
For when a mans at work in a field
Your glasses and pots no comfort will yield,
But a good leather bottell standing by
Will raise his spirits whenever he 's dry.

. . . .

And when the bottell at last grows old,
And will good liquor no longer hold,
Out of the side you may make a clout
To mend your shoes when they 're worn out,
Or take and hang it up on a pin
'T will serve to put hinges and odd things in.

Latten-ware was a kind of brass. It may be noted that no tin appears on this list, nor in many of the inventories of these early Connecticut colonists. Thomas Hooker had several "tynnen covers."

Brass utensils were far from cheap. Handsome brass mortars were expensive. Brass kettles were worth three pounds apiece. No wonder the Indians wished their brass kettles buried with them as their most precious possessions. The brass utensils of William Whiting, of Hartford, in 1649, were worth twenty pounds; Thomas Hooker's, about fifteen pounds. Among other utensils named in the inventories of some neighbors of

Mr. Hooker were an "iron to make Wafer cakes," "dyitt vessels," "shredin knife," "flesh fork." Robert Day had a "brass chaffin dish, 3s, lether bottle 2s, brass posnet 4s, brass pott 6s, brass kettle 2. 10s." A chafing-dish in olden times was an open box of wire into which coals were thrust.

Dame Huit, of Windsor, Conn., had these articles, among others : —

1 Cullender 2 Pudding pans. In kitchen in brasse & Iron potts, ladles, skimmers, dripping pans, posnets, and other pans........................ 6. 10s.

A pair Andirons 2 Brandii 2 Pair Crooks 3 pair of tonges and Iron Spitts pothangers........................... 1.

1 Fornace........................... 2.

Tubbs pales churnes butter barrels & other woodin implements........... 2.

The "two Brandii" were brand-irons or brond-yrons, a kind of trivet or support to set on the andirons. Sometimes they held brands or logs in place, or upon them dishes could be placed. Toasting-irons and broiling-irons are named. "Scieufes," or sieves, were worth a shilling apiece.

Eleazer Lusher, of Dedham, Mass., in 1672, owned cob-irons, trammels, firepans, gridirons, toasting-fork, salt pan, brand pan, mortar, pestle, box iron heaters, kettles, skillets, spits, frying-pan, ladles, skimmers, chafing-dishes, pots, pot-hooks, and creepers.

The name creeper brings to our consideration one of the homeliest charms of the fireplace — the andirons. Creepers were the lower and smaller andirons placed between the great firedogs. The word is also applied to a low cooking spider, which could be pushed in among the embers. Cob-irons were the simplest form of andirons, and usually were used merely to support the spit; sometimes they had hooks to hold a dripping-pan under the spit. Sometimes a fireplace showed three pairs of andirons, on which logs could be laid at various heights. Sometimes a single pair of andirons had three sets of hooks or branches for the same purpose. They were made of iron, copper, steel, or brass, often cast in a handsome design. The andirons played an important part in the construction and preservation of a fire.

And the construction of one of these great fires was no light or careless matter. Whit-

tier, in his *Snow-Bound*, thus tells of the
making of the fire in his home : —

> We piled with care our nightly stack
> Of wood against the chimney-back, —
> The oaken log, green, huge, and thick,
> And on its top the stout back-stick ;
> The knotty forestick laid apart,
> And filled between with curious art
> The ragged brush ; then hovering near
> We watched the first red blaze appear.

Often the great backlog had to be rolled
in with handspikes, sometimes drawn in by
a chain and yoke of oxen. The making of
the fire and its preservation from day to day
were of equal importance. The covering of
the brands at night was one of the domestic
duties, whose non-fulfillment in those match-
less days often rendered necessary a journey
with fire shovel to the house of the nearest
neighbor to obtain glowing coals to start
again the kitchen fire.

A domestic luxury seen in well-to-do homes
was a tin kitchen, a box-like arrangement
open on one side, which was set next the
blaze. It stood on four legs. In it bread
was baked or *roasted*. Through the kitchen
passed a spit, which could be turned by an

external handle ; on it meat was spitted to be roasted.

The brick oven was not used so frequently, usually but once a week. This was a permanent furnishing. When the great chimney was built, a solid heap of stones was placed for its foundation, and a vast and massive structure was reared upon it. On one side of the kitchen fireplace, but really a part of the chimney whole, was an oven which opened at one side into the chimney, and below an ash pit with swinging iron doors with a damper. To heat this oven a great fire of dry wood was kindled within it, and kept burning fiercely for some hours. Then the coal and ashes were removed, the chimney draught and damper were closed, and the food to be cooked was placed in the heated oven. Great pans of brown bread, pots of pork and beans, an Indian pudding, a dozen pies, all went into the fiery furnace together.

On Thanksgiving week the great oven was heated night and morning for several days. To place edibles at the rear of the glowing oven, it is plain some kind of a shovel must be used ; and an abnormally long-handled one was universally found by the oven-side. It was called a slice or peel, or fire-peel or bread-peel. Such an emblem was it of domestic utility and unity that a peel and a strong pair of tongs were a universal and luck-bearing gift to a bride. A good iron peel and tongs cost about a dollar and a half. The name occurs constantly in old wills among kitchen properties. We read of " the oven, the mawkin, the bavin, the peel." Sometimes, when the oven was heated, the peel was besprinkled with meal, and great heaps of rye and Indian dough were placed thereon, and by a dextrous and indescribable twist thrown upon cabbage leaves on the oven-bottom, and thus baked in a haycock shape.

" Shepherd Tom " Hazard, in his inimitable *Jonny Cake Papers*, thus speaks of the old-time methods of baking : —

Rhineinjun bread, vulgarly called nowadays rye and Indian bread, in the olden time was always made of one quart of unbolted Rhode Island rye meal to two quarts of the coarser grained parts of Ambrosia (Narragansett corn meal) well kneaded and made into large round loaves of the size of a half-peck measure. There are two ways of baking it. One way was to fill two large iron basins with the kneaded dough and, late in the evening, when the logs were well burned down, to clear a place in the middle of the fire and place the two basins of bread, one on top of the other, so as to inclose their contents and press them into one loaf. The whole was then carefully covered with hot ashes, with coals on top, and left until morning. Another way was to place a number of loaves in iron basins in a long-heated and well-tempered brick oven — stone would not answer as the heat is too brittle — into which a cup of water was also placed to make the crust soft. The difference between brown bread baked in this way, with its thick, soft, sweet crust, from that baked in the oven of an iron stove I leave to abler pens than mine to portray.

In friendly chimney corners there stood a jovial companion of the peel and tongs, the flip iron, or loggerhead, or flip-dog, or hottle. Lowell wrote : —

> Where dozed a fire of beechen logs that bred
> Strange fancies in its embers golden-red,
> And nursed the loggerhead, whose hissing dip,
> Timed by nice instinct, creamed the bowl of flip.

Flip was a drink of vast popularity, and I believe of potent benefit in those days when fierce winters and cold houses made hot drinks more necessary to the preservation of health than nowadays. I have drunk flip, but, like many a much-vaunted luxury of the olden time, I prefer to read of it. It is indescribably burnt and bitter in flavor.

It may be noted in nearly all old inventories that a warming-pan is a part of the kitchen furnishing. Wood wrote in 1634 of exportation to the New England colony, "Warming pannes & stewing pannes are of necessary use and very good traffick there." One was invoiced in 1642 at 3*s.* 6*d.*, another in 1654 at 5*s.* A warming-pan was a shallow pan of metal, usually brass or iron, about a foot in diameter and three or four inches deep, with a pierced brass or copper cover. It was fitted with a long wooden handle. When used, it was filled with coals, and when thoroughly heated, was thrust between the icy sheets of the bed, and moved up and down to give warmth to every corner. Its fireside neighbor was the footstove, a box of perforated metal in a wooden frame, within which hot coals could be placed to warm the feet of the goodwife during a long winter's drive, or to render endurable the arctic atmosphere of the unheated churches. Often a lantern of pierced metal hung near the warming-pan. The old-time lanterns, still occasionally found in New England kitchens or barns, form a most interesting study for the antiquary, and a much neglected fad for the collector. I have one of Elizabethan shape, to which, when I found it, fragments of thin sheets of horn still clung — the remains of the horn slides which originally were enclosed in the metal frame.

High up on the heavy beam over the fireplace stood usually a candlestick, an old lamp, perhaps a sausage stuffer, or a spice-mill, or a candle mold, a couple of wooden noggins, sometimes a pipe-tongs. By the side of the fireplace hung the soot-blackened, smoke-dried almanac, and near it often hung a betty-lamp, whose ill-smelling flame could supply for conning the pages a closer though scarce brighter light than the flickering hearth flame.

By the hearth, sometimes in the chimney corner, stood the high-backed settle, a sheltered seat, while the family dye-pot often was used by the children as a chimney bench.

Many household utensils once in common use in New England are now nearly obsolete. In many cases the old-time names are disused and forgotton, while the object itself may still be found with some modern appellation. In reading old wills, inventories, and enroll-ments, and the advertisements in old news-papers, I have made many notes of these old names, and have sometimes succeeded, though with difficulty, in identifying the utensils thus designated. Of course the different English shire dialects supply a va-riety of local names. In some cases good old English words have been retained in constant use in New England, while wholly archaïc in the fatherland.

In every thrifty New England home there stood a tub containing a pickle for salting meat. It was called a powdering-tub, or powdering-trough. This use of the word "powder" for salt dates even before Shake-speare's day.

Grains is an obsolete word for tines or prongs. Winthrop wrote in 1643 that a snake crawled in the Assembly room, and a parson "held it with his foot and staff with a small pair of grains and killed it."

Spenser used the word "flasket" thus : "In which to gather flowers to fill their flasket." It was a basket, or hamper, made of woven wicker. John Hull, writing in 1675, asks that "Wikker Flasketts" be brought to him on the *Sea Flower.*

A skeel was a small, shallow wooden tub, principally used for holding milk to stand for cream. It sometimes had one handle. The word is now used in Yorkshire. Akin to it is the word keeler, a small wooden tub, which is still constantly heard in New England, especially in application to a tub in which dishes are washed. Originally, cedar keelers were made to hold milk, and a losset was also a large flat wooden dish used for the same purpose. A skippet was a vessel much like a dipper, small and round, with long handle, and used for ladling liquids.

A quarn was a hand-mill for grinding meal, and sometimes it stood in a room by itself. It was a step in domestic progress beyond pounding grain with a pestle in a mortar, and was of earlier date than the windmill or water-mill. In Wiclif's translation we read in Matthew xxiv : " Two wymmen schalen be gryndynge in quern," etc. This word is also used by Shakespeare in *Midsummer Night's Dream.* In early New England wills the word is found, as in one of 1671 : " I paire Quarnes and Lumber in the quarne house, 10*s.*" It was sometimes spelled " cairn," as in a Windham will, and also "quern" and "quirn."

Sometimes a most puzzling term will be found in one of these old inventories, one which appears absolutely incomprehensible. Here is one which seems like a riddle of which the answer is irrevocably lost : " One Billy bassha Pan." It is found in the kitchen list of the rich possessions of Madam De Peyster, in 1774, which inventory is pre-served, in the family archives at the Van Cortlandt Manor House, at Croton-on-Hudson. You can give any answer you please to the riddle ; but my answer is this, in slightly altered verse. I think that Madam De Peyster's cook used that dish to serve : —

> A sort of soup or broth or stew
> Or hotchpot of all sorts of fishes,
> That Greenwich never could outdo,
> Green herbs, red peppers, mussels, saffron,

Soles, onions, garlic, roach and dace ;
All these were cooked in the Manor kitchen,
In that one dish of Bouillabaisse.

The early settlers were largely indebted to
various forest trees for cheap, available, and
utilizable material for the manufacture of
both kitchen utensils and tableware. Wood-
turning was for many years a recognized
trade; dish-turner a business title. We find
Lion Gardiner writing to John Winthrop,
Jr., in 1652, " My wyfe desireth Mistress
Lake to get her a dozen of trays for shee
hearith that there is a good tray-maker with
you."

Governor Bradford found the Indians using
wooden bowls, trays, and dishes, and the " Indian bowls," made from the knots of maple-
trees, were much sought after by housekeep-
ers till this century. A fine specimen of
these bowls is now in the Massachusetts
Historical Society. It was originally taken
from the wigwam of King Philip. Wooden
noggins (low bowls with handles) are constantly named in early inventories, and Mary
Ring, of Plymouth, thought, in 1633, that a
" wodden cupp " was valuable enough to
leave by will as a token of friendship.

Wooden trenchers, also made by hand, were used on the table for more than a century, and were universally bequeathed by will, as by that of Miles Standish. White poplar wood made specially handsome dishes. Wooden pans were made in which to set milk. Wooden bread troughs were used in every home. These were oblong, trencher-shaped bowls, about a foot and a half in length, hollowed and shaped by hand from a log of wood. Across the trough ran lengthwise a stick or rod, on which the flour was sifted in a temse, or searce, or sieve. The saying, "set the Thames on fire," is said to have been originally "set the temse on fire," meaning that hard labor would, by the friction of constant turning, set the wooden temse, or sieve, on fire.

It was not necessary to apply to the wood-turner to manufacture these simply shaped dishes. Every winter the men and boys of the household manufactured every kind of domestic utensils and portions of farm implements that could be whittled or made from wood with simple tools. By the cheerful kitchen fireside much of this work was done. Indeed, the winter picture of the fireside

should always show the figure of a whittling
boy. They made butter paddles of red
cherry, salt mortars, pig troughs, pokes, sled
neaps, ax helves, which were sawn, whittled,
and carefully scraped with glass ; box traps
and "figure 4" traps, noggins, keelers, rund-
lets, flails, cheese-hoops, cheese-ladders, stan-
chions, handles for all kinds of farm implements, and niddy-noddys. Strange to say,
the latter word is not found in any of our
dictionaries, though the word is as well
known in country vernacular as the article
itself — a hand-reel — or as the old riddle : —

> Niddy-noddy,
> Two heads and one body.

There were still other wooden vessels. In
his *Philocothonista, or The Drunkard Opened,
Dissected and Anatomized* (1635), Thomas
Heywood, gives for "carouseing-bowles of
wood" these names : "mazers, noggins, whis-
kins, piggins, cruizes, wassel-bowles, ale-
bowles, court-dishes, tankards, kannes."

There were many ways of usefully em-
ploying the winter evening hours. Some
thrifty folk a hundred years ago occupied
spare time in sticking card-teeth in wool-

cards. The strips of pierced leather and the wire teeth bent in proper shape were supplied to them by the card manufacturer. The long leather strips and boxes filled with the bent wire teeth might be seen standing in many a country home, and many an evening by the light of the blazing fire, — for the work required little eyesight or dexterity, — sat the children on dye-pot, crickets, and logs of wood, earning a scant sum to add to their "broom-money."

By the side of the chimney, in New England country houses, always hung a broom or besom of peeled birch. These birch brooms were a characteristic New England production. To make one a straight birch-tree from three to four inches in diameter was chosen, and about five feet of the trunk was cut off. Ten inches from the larger end a notch was cut around the stick, and the bark peeled off from thence to the end. Then with a sharp knife the bared end was carefully split up to the notch in slender slivers, which were held back by the broom-maker's left hand until they became too many and too bulky to restrain, when they were tied back with a string. As the tendency of the slivers or splints was to grow slightly thinner toward the notch, there was left in the heart of the growing broom a short core, which had to be whittled off. When this was done the splints were all turned back to their first and natural position, a second notch was cut an inch above the first one, leaving a strip of bark an inch in diameter; the bark was peeled off from what was destined to be the broom handle, and a series of splints was shaved down toward the second notch. Enough of the stick was left to form the handle; this was carefully whittled until an inch or so in diameter, was smoothed, and furnished with a hole in the end in which to place a string or a strip of leather for suspension. The second series of splints from the handle end was firmly turned down and tied with hempen twine over the wholly splintered end, and all the splints cut off the same length. The inch of bark which remained of the original tree helped to hold the broom-splints firmly in place.

When these brooms were partly worn, the restraining string could be removed, and the flaring splints formed an ideal oven-besom, spreading and cleaning the ashes from every

corner and crevice. Corn brooms were unknown in these country neighborhoods until
about the middle of the present century.

A century, and even as late as half a century ago, many a farmer's son (and daughter
too) throughout New England earned his or
her first spending-money by making birch
brooms for the country stores, from whence
they were sent to the large cities, especially
Boston, where there was a constant demand
for them. In Northampton, about 1790, one
shopkeeper kept as many as seven or eight
hundred of these brooms on hand at one
time.

The boys and girls did not grow rich very
fast at broom-making. Throughout Ver-
mont, fifty years ago, the uniform price paid
to the maker for these brooms was but six
cents apiece, and as he had to work at least
three evenings to make one broom, — to say
nothing of the time spent in selecting and
cutting the birch-tree, — it was not so profitable an industry as gathering beech-nuts
at a dollar a bushel. Major Robert Randolph
told in fashionable London circles, that
about the year 1750, he carried many a
loadof these birch brooms on his back ten

miles to Concord, that he might thus earn a few shillings. Such brooms were known by different names in different localities : birch brooms, splinter brooms, and Indian brooms. The Indians were very proficient in making them, and it is said invented them. This can readily be believed, for like birch-bark canoes and snowshoes, they are examples of perfection in utility and in the employment of native materials. Squaws wandered over certain portions of the country bearing brooms on their backs, peddling them from house to house for ninepence apiece and a drink of cider. In 1806, one minister of Haverhill, New Hampshire, had two of these brooms given to him as a marriage fee. When a Hadley man planted broom corn in 1797, and made corn brooms to sell, he was scornfully met with the remark that broom-making was work for Indians and boys. It was long ere his industry crowded out the sturdy birch brooms.

There were many domestic duties which did not waft sweet "odors of Araby;" the annual spring manufacture of soft soap for home consumption was one of them, and also one of the most important and most trying of all the household industries. The refuse grease from the family cooking was stowed away in tubs and barrels through the cool winter months in unsavory masses, and the wood-ashes from the great fireplaces were also thriftily stored until the carefully chosen time arrived. The day was selected with much deliberation, after close consultation with that family counselor, the almanac, for the moon must be in the right quarter, and the tide at the flood, if the soap were to "come right." Then the leach was was set outside the kitchen door. Some families owned a strongly made leach-tub, some used a barrel, others cut a section from a great birch-tree, and removed the bark to form a tub, which was placed loosely in a circular groove in a base made of wood or, preferably, of stone. This was not set horizontally, but was slightly inclined. The tub was filled with ashes, and water was scantily poured in until the lye trickled or leached out of an outlet cut in the groove at the base. The "first run" of lye was not strong enough to be of use, and was poured again upon the ashes. The wasted ashes were replenished again and again, and water poured in small quantities on them, and the lye accumulated in a receptacle placed for it. It was a universal test that when the lye was strong enough to hold up an egg, it was also strong enough to use for the soap boiling. In the largest iron pot the grease and lye were boiled together, often over a great fire built in the open air. The leached ashes were not deemed refuse and waste; they were used by the farmer as a fertilizer. Soap made in this way, while rank and strong, is so pure and clean that it seems almost like a jelly, and shows no trace of the vile grease that helped to form it.

The dancing firelight shone out on no busier scene than on the grand candle-dipping. It had taken weeks to prepare for this domestic industry, which was the great household event of the late autumn, as soapmaking was of the spring. Tallow had been carefully saved from the domestic animals killed on the farm, the honeyed store of the patient bee had been robbed of wax to furnish materials, and there was still another source of supply.

The summer air of the coast of New England still is sweet with one of the freshest,

purest plant-perfumes in the world — the
scent of bayberry. These dense woody
shrubs bear profusely a tiny, spicy, wax-
coated berry; and the earliest colonists
quickly learned that from this plentiful berry
could be obtained an inflammable wax, which
would replace and supplement any lack of
tallow. The name so universally applied to
the plant — candleberry — commemorates its
employment for this purpose. I never pass
the clumps of bayberry bushes in the early
autumn without eagerly picking and crush-
ing the perfumed leaves and berries; and
the clean, fresh scent seems to awaken a
dim recollection, — a hereditary memory, —
and I see, as in a vision, the sober little children of the Puritans standing in the clear
glowing sunlight, and faithfully stripping
from the gnarled bushes the waxy candle-
berries; not only affording through this occupation material assistance to the household
supplies, but finding therein health, and I
am sure happiness, if they loved the bay-
berries as I, their descendant, do.

The method of preparing this wax was
simple; it still exists in a few Plymouth
County households. The berries are simply

boiled with hot water in a kettle, and the resolved wax skimmed off the top, refined, and permitted to harden into cakes or candles. The references in old-time records to this bayberry wax are too numerous to be recounted. A Virginian governor, Robert Beverley (for the bayberry and its wax was known also in the South as myrtleberry wax), gave, perhaps, the clearest description of it : —

A pale green brittle wax of a curious green color, which by refining becomes almost transparent. Of this they made candles which are never greasy to the touch nor melt with lying in the hottest weather; neither does the snuff of these ever offend the smell, like that of a tallow candle ; but instead of being disagreeable, if an accident puts a candle out, it yields a pleasant fragrancy to all that are in the room ; insomuch that nice people often put them out on purpose to have the incense of the expiring snuff.

It is true that the balmy breath of the bayberry is exhaled even on its funeral pyre. A bayberry candle burns like incense ; and I always think of its perfume as truly the incense to the household hearth-gods of an old New England home.

Bayberry wax was a standard farm-product, a staple article of traffic, till this century, and it was constantly advertised in the newspapers. As early as 1712, Thomas Lechmere wrote to John Winthrop, Jr. : —

I am now to beg one favour of you, that you secure for me all the bayberry wax you can possibly lay yor hands on. What charge you shall be at securing it shall be thankfully paid you. You must take a care that they do not putt too much tallow among it, being a custome and cheate they have gott.

When the candle-dipping began, a fierce fire was built in the fireplace, and over it was hung the largest house kettle, half filled with water and melted tallow, or wax. Candle-rods were brought down from the attic, or pulled out from under the edge of beams, and placed about a foot and a half apart, reaching from chair to chair.

Boards were placed underneath to save the spotless floor from greasy drippings. Across these rods were laid, like the rounds of a ladder, shorter sticks or reeds to which the wicks were attached at intervals of a few inches. The wicks of loosely spun cotton or tow were dipped time and time again into the melted tallow, and left to harden between each dipping. Of course, if the end of the kitchen (where stood the rods and hung the wicks) were very cold, the candles grew quickly, since they hardened quickly; but they were then more apt to crack. When they were of proper size, they were cut off, spread in a sunny place in the garret to bleach, and finally stored away in candle-boxes. Sometimes the tallow was poured into molds; when, of course, comparatively few candles could be made in a day. In some communities itinerant candle-makers carried molds from house to house, and assisted in the candle manufacture.

These candles were placed in candle-sticks, or in large rooms were set in rude chandeliers of strips of metal with sockets, called candle-beams. Handsome rooms had sconces, and the kitchen often had a sliding stand by which the candle could be adjusted at a desired height. Snuffers were as indispensable as candlesticks, and were sometimes called snuffing-iron, or snit — a word not in the *Century Dictionary* — from the old English verb, "snyten," to blow out. The snuffers lay in a little tray called a snuffertray, snuffer-dish, snuffer-boat, snuffer-slice, or snuffer-pan. Save-alls, a little wire frame to hold up the last burning end of candle, were another contrivance of our frugal ancestors.

In no way was a thrifty housewife better known than through her abundant stock of symmetrical candles; and nowhere was a skilful and dextrous hand more needed than in shaping them. Still, candles were not very costly if the careless housewife chose to purchase them. The *Boston Evening Post* of October 5, 1767, has this advertisement: "Dip'd Tallow Candles Half a Pistareen the single Pound & Cheaper by Cwt."

In many a country household some old-time frugalities linger, but the bounteous oil-wells of Pennsylvania have rendered candles not only obsolete, but too costly for country use, and by a turn of fashion they have become comparatively an article of luxury, but still seem to throw an old-time refinement wherever their soft rays shine.

An account of housewifely duties in my great-grandmother's home was thus written, in halting rhyme, by one of her sons when he too was old: —

The boys dressed the flax, the girls spun the tow,
The music of mother's footwheel was not slow.
The flax on the bended pine distaff was spread,
With squash shell of water to moisten the thread.
Such were the pianos our mothers did keep
Which they played on while spinning their children to
    sleep.
My mother I 'm sure must have borne off the medal,
For she always was placing her foot on the pedal.
The warp and the filling were piled in the room,
Till the web was completed and fit for the loom,
Then labor was pleasure, and industry smiled,
And the wheel and the loom every trouble beguiled,
And there at the distaff the good wives were made.
Thus Solomon's precepts were fully obeyed.

The manufacture of the farm-reared wool
was not so burdensome and tedious a process as that of flax, but it was far from
pleasant. The fleeces of wool had to be
opened out and cleaned of all sticks, burrs,
leaves, feltings, tar-marks, and the dirt which
always remained after months' wear by the
sheep; then it had to be sorted out for
dyeing, which latter was a most unpleasant
process. Layers of the various colors of
wools after being dyed were rolled together
and carded on coarse wool-cards, again and
again, then slightly greased by a disagreeable and tiresome method, then run into
rolls. The wool was spun on the great wheel

which stood in the kitchen with the reel and swifts, and often by the glowing firelight the mother spun. A tender and beautiful picture of this domestic scene has been drawn by Dr. Gurdon Russell, of Hartford, in his *Up Neck in 1825.*

My mother was spinning with the great wheel, the white rolls of wool lay upon the platform, and as they were spun upon the spindle, she turning the wheel with one hand, and with extended arm and delicate fingers holding the roll in the other, stepping backwards and forwards lightly till it was spun into yarn, it formed a picture to me, sitting upon a low stool, which can never be forgotten. Her movements were every grace, her form all of beauty to me who opposite sat and was watching her dextrous fingers.

The manufacture of flax into linen material was ever felt to be of vast importance, and was encouraged by legislation from earliest colonial days, but it received a fresh impulse in New England through the immigration of about one hundred Irish families from Londonderry. They settled in New Hampshire on the Merrimac about 1719. They spun and wove by hand, but with far more skill than prevailed among those English settlers who had already become Americans. They established a manufactory according to Irish methods, and attempts at a similar establishment were made in Boston. There was much public excitement over spinning. Women, rich as well as poor, appeared on Boston Common with their wheels, thus making spinning a popular holiday recreation. A brick building was erected as a spinning-school, and a tax was placed in 1737 to support it. But this was not an industrial success, the excitement died out, the public spinning-school lost its ephemeral popularity, and the wheel became again simply a domestic duty and pride.

For many years after this, housewives had everywhere flax and hemp to spin and weave in their homes, and the preparation of these staples seems to us to-day a monumental labor. On almost every farm might be seen a patch of the pretty flax, ripening for the hard work of pulling, rippling, rotting, breaking, swingling, and combing, which all had to be done before it came to the women's hands for spinning. The seed was sown broadcast, and allowed to grow till the bobs or bolls were ripe. The flax was then pulled and spread neatly in rows to dry. This work could be done by boys. Then men whipped or threshed or rippled out all the seed to use for meal; afterwards the flax stalks were allowed to lie for some time in water until the shives were thoroughly rotten, when they were cleaned and once more thoroughly dried and tied in bundles. Then came work for strong men, to break the flax on the ponderous flaxbreak, to get out the hard "hexe" or "bun," and to swingle it with a swingle knife, which was somewhat like a wooden dagger. Active men could swingle forty pounds a day on the swingling-board. It was then hetchelled or combed or hackled by the housewife, and thus the rough tow was gotten out, when it was straightened and made ready for the spruce distaff, round which it was finally wrapped. The hatchelling was tedious work and irritating to the lungs, for the air was filled with the fluffy particles which penetrated everywhere. The thread was then spun on a "little wheel." It was thought that to spin two double skeins of linen, or four double skeins of tow, or to weave six yards of linen, was a good day's work. For a week's work a girl received fifty cents and "her keep." She thus got less than a cent and a half a yard for weaving. The skeins of linen thread went through many tedious processes of washing and bleaching before being ready for weaving; and after the cloth was woven it was "bucked" in a strong lye, time and time again, and washed out an equal number of times. Then it was "belted" with a maple beetle on a smooth, flat stone; then washed and spread out to bleach in the pure sunlight. Sometimes the thread, after being spun and woven, had been washed and belted a score of times ere it was deemed white and soft enough to use. The little girls could spin the "swingling tow" into coarse twine, and the older ones make "all tow" and "tow and linen" and "harden" stuffs to sell.

To show the various duties attending the manufacture of these domestic textiles by a Boston woman of intelligence and social standing, as late as 1788, let me quote a few entries from the diary of the wife of Col. John May : —

A large kettle of yarn to attend upon. Lucretia and self rinse our through many waters, get out, dry, attend to, bring in, do up and sort 110 score of yarn, this with baking and ironing.

Went to hackling flax.

Rose early to help Ruth warp and put a piece in the loom.

Baking and hackling yarn. A long web of tow to whiten and weave.

The wringing out of this linen yarn was most exhausting, and the rinsing in various waters was no simple matter in those days, for the water did not conveniently run into the houses through pipes and conduits, but had to be laboriously carried in pailfuls from a pump, or more frequently raised in a bucket from a well.

I am always touched, when handling the homespun linens of olden times, with a sense that the vitality and strength of those enduring women, through the many tedious and exhausting processes which they had bestowed, were woven into the warp and woof with the flax, and gave to the old webs of linen their permanence and their beautiful texture. How firm they are, and how lustrous! And how exquisitely quaint and fine

are their designs; sometimes even Scriptural
designs and lessons are woven into them.
They are, indeed, a beautiful expression of
old-time home and farm life. With their
close-woven, honest threads runs this finer
beauty, which may be impalpable and imper-
ceptible to a stranger, but which to me is
real and ever-present, and puts me truly in
touch with the life of my forbears. But,
alas, it is through intuition we must learn of
this old-time home life, for it has vanished
from our sight, and much that is beautiful
and good has vanished with it.

The associations of the kitchen fireside
that linger in the hearts of those who are
now old can find no counterpart in our
domestic surroundings to-day. The welcome
cheer of the open fire, which graced and
beautified even the humblest room, is lost
forever with the close gatherings of the
family, the household occupations, the homespun industries which formed and imprinted in the mind of every
child the picture of
a home.